The Splintered Soul

The Splintered Soul

Shamanic Journeys to
Heal the Inner Darkness

Maryanne Clare

for the evolving human spirit

HAMPTON ROADS
PUBLISHING COMPANY, INC.

Cover art by Randall Rozzell
Cover design by Marjoram Productions

For information write:

Hampton Roads Publishing Company, Inc.
134 Burgess Lane
Charlottesville, VA 22902

Or call: (804)296-2772
FAX: (804)296-5096
e-mail: hrpc@hrpub.com
Web site: http://www.hrpub.com

If you are unable to order this book from your local bookseller, you
may order directly from the publisher.
Quantity discounts for organizations are available.
Call 1-800-766-8009, toll-free.

ISBN 1-57174-070-8

10 9 8 7 6 5 4 3 2 1

Printed on acid-free paper in the
United States of America

Preface

This story would be difficult for me to believe if it had not happened to me. I have no proof of its authenticity except for what I have felt in the core of my being: that is the place of my truth, and it is a very subjective view, I'll grant. But how does anyone really know truth outside of what they feel inside their own heart? So if you have doubts as you read my words, be assured that a part of me has been doubting and denying every step of the way. It has been a struggle to learn to trust what I have felt inside my heart, as my mind has tried to convince me of the absurdity of what was revealed to me.

Auschwitz

The morning of the day we decided to go to Auschwitz I felt myself wanting to procrastinate, wanting to find a reason not to go. Only with the help of my friend did the moment of weakness pass, and I mustered the strength and courage to face this task.

The train ride from Krakow to Auschwitz, or Oświęcim, the Polish name for this town, took about an hour. It was a slow ride, past farmland and small towns. The landscape was very pastoral with green rolling hills. Such a peaceful place for a death camp!

Arriving at Oświęcim station I felt such heaviness in the air. I was surprised to find that there was actually a town here. But why shouldn't there be? The German name of Auschwitz originated with the concentration camp. But the town of Oświęcim existed before the camp and would continue to exist after.

We disembarked and made our way to the station. There were no obvious signs as to where the camp was, but there was a tour bus that would take you there. No way, I decided, was I going to ride with a group of people on some kind of transport to Auschwitz—I had to go as an individual. A choice clearly my own. Any hint of the way people were brought there in the past I wanted no part of. The knowledge of the masses of people herded there by train was enough. I did not want to reenact the scene in any way.

So we started walking west down the road that passed the train station, simply allowing our intuition to guide us. The intense energy of Auschwitz could not be missed. We rounded a turn and began to head south and soon came upon a set of abandoned railroad tracks. No accident here. Just put one foot in front of the other and follow the track, I told myself. As we drew closer, this became increasingly easier said than done. The walk was only a few miles. But the closer we got, the harder it was for me to keep pace.

It wasn't long before Heidi, who was able to keep a steady pace, was thirty to forty feet in front of me, and I had to struggle to catch up. In fact, I couldn't. Being slightly embarrassed, I finally had to ask her to slow down.

It was the same as it had been in Berlin. All around me was calm and peace, but my inner experience was filled with dread. I knew I was about to enter the gates of hell and that I could turn around and run away. Sometimes that was the hardest thing—the knowledge that I could leave, that I didn't have to do this, to choose to walk into the darkness. I have amazed myself that more than once I have found the courage to enter.

When we were within a half mile of the camp, on the right side of the road behind barbed wire fencing was what seemed to be a long-abandoned factory. The area it covered seemed huge. From the road I couldn't see where it ended. And I remembered that I.G. Farben had used slave labor from the camp to run its factory near here, and I realized that this must be it. It felt very weird to see it just standing there looking innocent. And I was also amazed when I remembered that this factory had been a target for Allied bombing; how could the Allies have been so accurate as to hit this and not Auschwitz just a short distance away?

I remembered reading how the prisoners in the camp were so happy when the air raids began. They were filled with joy at the destruction raining down. And I remember one man saying how he actually didn't feel fear from the bombs. I guess because it somehow represented to him the possibility that someone might actually defeat the Germans after all, which would mean survival and freedom for him.

The railroad tracks guided us to our destination. A parking lot—odd. But that's how it is now. A parking lot and then the reception building. Bookstore, refreshments, money exchange, bathrooms, and the movie theater. Most of the movie footage was made by the Soviets at the time of the liberation—dated black-and-white film but graphic. You get the point.

And then we stepped out into a courtyard, and standing before us was the guardhouse adjacent to the infamous gate, "Arbeit Macht Frei" (Work Will Set You Free). And the rows of brick buildings in the background behind the barbed wire fences. It was here, standing on the outside looking in, that my emotions overcame me. The immensity of my guilt took over, and I began to cry from deep within me. I could go no further. Once again I wished, of course pointlessly, that it had never happened and wondered how was I possibly going to face this hard evidence.

How could I possibly walk this hallowed ground? I almost felt that I could not be worthy. Would the souls of the dead prisoners allow me in this space? Would they believe that I, SS Sergeant Hans Grunewald, was here for healing and forgiveness? Could they believe that? Could I believe that? Could I believe that I could be forgiven? The only way I would know would be to walk through that gate and enter.

It took me several minutes to compose myself. I hadn't come this far not to continue on. Feeling shaky and weak, but with my strong friend by my side I entered the gate. And somewhere in my being, although not fully conscious at this time, I knew the truth of the gate would be revealed to me. My work would set me free.

I walked through the gate, and on the right was the building that was the kitchen. It was against this outer wall that the camp orchestra had played as the inmates walked through this gate to their labor in the early morning hours and again when they would return at night, fewer in number. We continued on down the unpaved road. Most of the roads that I saw between the buildings were unpaved. The dirt was hard now, but I remember reading how thick in mud these roads could be and how so many prisoners suffered from frostbite, as their foot coverings were very inadequate. Most of them wore wooden shoes and some were even barefoot!

The camp was laid out very orderly, with row upon row of two-story brick buildings. This part of the camp was not created by the Germans but was initially a Polish army barracks. The Germans simply made use of the existing buildings and then added what they needed. Large trees were scattered throughout the grounds. It was April and they were just coming into bloom and the birds were singing. The weather was very pleasant. But the energy I felt would not be swayed by the pleasant external circumstances.

We had a guidebook for the camp that took us on a walking tour. I have that book with me now, and the memory of being there is as fresh as the memory of this morning. Urging myself to reread the information is taking great strength from me. I guess it is in a moment like this when I realize just why Auschwitz should not be torn down. My first reaction to this place was to tear it down so that evil would then be eradicated. But with time, I have realized that destroying the evidence of evil does not heal. Nor does it destroy evil. Every human being should see the darkness that exists in the human soul; maybe then we might not do this again. But unfortunately I feel rather pessimistic about this. And I see how strong within me is the desire to turn away from this truth, this tragedy. I don't want to look. I don't want to believe.

Well, as we continued on our journey through Auschwitz other people were there too, of course, and many were in groups. I found that I had to avoid being anywhere near a group of people while moving through the camp. Every time I see in my mind's eye one of those groups of tourists walking through the buildings, or especially down one of the roads, I feel a chill and have difficulty breathing. It is too close to the images of the past.

The buildings that housed the prisoners fifty years ago are now used as exhibit rooms. In one are piles of personal possessions that were confiscated upon arrival: thousands of wire-rimmed spectacles...hundreds of shoes...suitcases with people's names and addresses printed on them...toothbrushes... hair brushes...hundreds of artificial limbs, legs mostly. And human hair...huge mounds of female hair, even some with the long braids still in them. And in one exhibit is the human hair that was woven into hair cloth. The sheer number of the human possessions slowly brought on the effect of the enormity of it all. And what is displayed in this one building is minuscule compared with the huge booty the Nazis actually confiscated.

In another cell block is a description of what happened to the people when they were brought into the camp. Ninety percent of arrivals were gassed immediately. Those who survived the initial selection then had their personal possessions taken; their hair was cut and they were sprayed with disinfectant, bathed, given a number, and registered.

They were given the infamous blue-and-white striped clothing, which made them an easy target if they were to try to escape. Sewn on the clothing was a symbol that placed each inmate in a certain category. Mostly these were different-colored triangles (the Jewish people, of course, had their yellow star.) The color red was for political prisoners and Communists, black for gypsies and those viewed as antisocial by the Nazis, violet for Jehovah's Witnesses, and pink for homosexuals. I often wonder how many gay people who proudly wear the pink triangle now have any idea what its origin was.

Lining the corridors of the cell blocks were pictures of inmates, portraits almost. Eight by tens, taken when they were first brought in. Their heads were shaved, and most of them were wearing the blue-and-white striped uniforms. Their shaven heads stripped them not only of their individuality but also their sexuality. Often it was difficult to tell if someone was a man or a woman. Here the men looked softer and the women looked harder. But some women looked so soft you could almost see through them. They haunt me still. I see their faces in my dreams. The fear and shock is so alive in their faces. The prisoners look like anyone's mother,

13

grandmother, brother, father. They can't believe what has happened. One moment they were living normal, perhaps mundane lives, and then all of a sudden evil was unleashed that was so inhuman, so cold, so uncaring.

In the midst of the unbelievable fear and shock, one woman smiles as if in perfect reflex response to a lifetime of picture-taking. And I look back at her, unbelieving. This image is recorded for eternity. What does a smile mean? Perhaps with all else lost, a smile is the only thing left? Maybe it is a sign of God. For who could smile in this tragedy? Who could turn the other cheek but someone of God? God himself. God as she is. What was done to this smiling God in this hell?

The halls of the blocks are lined with these photographs. Hundreds of them. Recorded along with the prisoners' names and dates of birth were the dates they were brought into the camp and their length of survival. Most had stayed in the camp for only a few weeks to a few months. It's hard to realize that so many, most in fact, were only there for a short time. Maybe in one way this was a blessing in that they had to endure this hell only briefly. But their image at the moment the devil descended upon the earth was recorded forever.

Leaving these halls lined with the faces of the ghosts of the past, I entered through a wooden gate and stood in an open gravel courtyard. At the far end was a wall. At the base of the wall were hundreds of colored flowers and small candles with flames flickering in the gentle breeze. I was facing the "wall of death," the execution wall, which was made of cork so as to muffle the sound of the bullets as they passed through the prisoners.

I slowly made my way to the wall. I had brought a candle with me, and this seemed like the place to leave it. I also had brought with me several crystals that I had used in journeys to help me see into the darkness of my past. I brought them with me to leave in this place of hell and darkness so that those souls that still remained might be able to use them as a way out of the dark and into the light. I placed one of these crystals in a small space in the cork wall.

As I stood before this place I felt emotions that I now find difficult to describe. A place within me was touched deeply, and I could feel that my presence here was enough. There would be no words that I could say that would equal the power of simply standing before this wall and praying to God and asking him to be here.

After pausing for a few minutes of deep reflection and prayer, my tour of Auschwitz continued. The courtyard with the execution wall was directly adjacent to cell block 11. This was called the "death block." It was here the prisoners were held for torture and punishment. I will describe the main points of what I remember of this block. It was very difficult for me to be there. On the ground floor were small prison cells and some holding areas. It was down here in one of the holding areas that the first attempt at using the gas cyclon B for mass murder was made. It was used on several hundred Soviet prisoners and some of the sick from the hospital in 1941. There were also small cells that were used to hold anywhere from one to twenty prisoners depending on the punishment. The ventilation was so poor in these cells that some people literally suffocated to death.

But the place that stands out the most in my memory was the room that held what was called the standing cells. I am claustrophobic, so this greatly affected me. These were four small cubicles that measured approximately one square yard. In each one would be placed four people undergoing special punishment. They were sent to labor all day and then forced to stand all night in these cells and then back to work the next day. This could go on for days. I placed a crystal here, although I was barely able to reach in far enough to do it. The energy was intense.

I got out of that block as fast as I could. Outside I was breathing hard and taking in the fresh air of the spring day and trying to stop myself from shaking. I was becoming very aware of the energy in different areas of the camp: I found there were places I could enter and others where it was as if a strong hand gripped my shoulder, pulled me back, and said, "No, don't go in there!" Walking away from Block 11 was a relief. I had to get away from there.

As we continued down the road, we came to the gallows on our left. It was very long and several people could be hanged at once. I wanted to place a crystal in the ground beneath the gallows, but as I approached to within a few feet of it, it was as if I had hit a wall and I could go no further. Heidi was able to transcend this invisible wall, and she buried the crystal for me as I watched. I was a little frustrated that I couldn't do it myself, but there was no denying the energetic feeling for me, and there was nothing I could do. So I thanked her and we moved on.

In the few hours that we spent at Auchwitz, I found it difficult to talk. It was so incredibly unreal to even be here that to try to have a regular conversation or convey what I was thinking and feeling was impossible. Heidi was very supportive of me and seemed to know that I needed to be left to my thoughts. I greatly appreciated her presence. She had volunteered to come with me to this place, and I was truly blessed by that.

The one comforting thought that pervaded my consciousness during the entire time was from the Twenty-third Psalm, "Yea, though I walk through the valley of the shadow of death, I will fear no evil." I kept saying it over and over to myself.

The next stop on the tour was the gas chamber with the crematorium. It was an interesting structure with a roof of earth that seemed to be built down into the ground, and I realized that what presented itself before me was a recreation of the original. In their frantic escape at the end of the war, the Nazis tried to destroy the physical evidence of their evil work, and so the original structure had been blown up and left in ruins. I had read that after the war there was a great debate as to whether this building of death should actually be rebuilt, and in the end it was. I think it was the right choice.

The structure was just standing there, with no signs as to how to enter. I spent a bit of time on the outside readying myself, then buried another crystal in the earthen roof. I went back down to the ground level and saw an open door. I walked up to it and looked in. I felt as if I had lost my air. I couldn't go in. The density I felt in there overwhelmed me, and I pulled my head out of the doorway. It was gray and dark inside and felt very cold.

I walked away once again, trying to regain my composure and catch my breath. I walked around the outside of the structure and poked my head in at the doorway at the opposite end. Here was the crematorium. I saw the furnaces. So the other door I had approached was the room where the prisoners were mur-dered—the "shower room." The darkness that lingered there was palpable. I walked away from the crematorium and found a place to sit about 100 feet away. I had lost track of Heidi.

It was here that I pulled out the little Bible my mother had given me for this trip, as I clutched the crucifix she had also given me—the one that was blessed by the Pope in 1940. With tears in my eyes I began reading the Twenty-third Psalm:

> *The Lord is my shepherd. I shall not want. He makes me to lie down in green pastures. He leads me beside the still waters. He restores my soul; He leads me in the paths of righteousness for His name's sake. Yea, though I walk through the valley of the shadow of death, I will fear no evil; For You are with me; Your rod and Your staff they comfort me. You prepare a table before me in the presence of my enemies; You anoint my head with oil; my cup runs over. Surely goodness and mercy shall follow me all the days of my life; and I will dwell in the house of the Lord forever.*

I read this over and over. Then I looked up and saw what seemed a miracle. In the time that I had sat down to read, several groups of tourists came through this place. And I watched them enter one by one on the side of the gas chamber. And then after a little while I saw them exit one by one on the side of the crematorium. They had no idea what they were throwing in the face of evil. But I did. The light was winning. Maybe this is part of the healing. All the tourists coming here one by one are creating a healing by walking into the gas chamber and walking out of the crematorium alive. It was not what this building had been designed for, but in the end, the truth would be that each person, aware or not, would walk away changed and more enlightened for having had the courage to enter this death chamber. And the thought came—maybe these people are the victims reincarnated thumbing their noses at the Nazis and ultimately, death.

Heidi finally found me and we smiled. Not much could be said after all of this. We both felt pretty drained and decided it was time to leave. We found a bench in the parking lot and sat for a while to rest before walking back to the train station.

We found it interesting to observe the people coming and going from this place. It was very easy to tell who had just arrived and who had just been in the camp. The arrivals were very light and joking and having fun with each other. A lot of talking going on. The people who had just walked through the camp were silent, and their expressions revealed sadness, disbelief, and mostly shock. It was an amazing thing to sit and observe the differences.

As for myself, the enormity of it all engulfed me. Auschwitz was so huge, and so many people were murdered there. I began to feel that I couldn't bear this enormous burden by myself. It was too much. Too much.

.1.

From a very early age I was fascinated with the events of World War II. My father was a career officer in the United States Army and had served in the war. Afterward, we lived in New Jersey, where I was born in 1958. We had a book called *Time's Picture History of World War II.* I would spend hours slowly leafing through the pages. Staring at each picture for several minutes, I couldn't take my eyes away. I felt possessed by those scenes.

I remember a picture of London rescue workers digging people out of the rubble after a bombing raid. The people were completely covered with dust and had blank, dazed looks on their faces. Splintered wood and shattered bricks and plaster lay about. I could feel the gritty dust from the rubble in my mouth. It was hard to imagine how that scene could have once been orderly. It was hard to imagine that it was probably orderly now, with every brick and piece of wood back in place.

Another picture I remember well was of a dead German soldier. He was lying face down by his burning tank. His left arm was blown off at the shoulder and rested near his body. I felt sorry for him. He seemed so young.

I would gaze endlessly at these scenes and ponder how it all could have happened. Who were these people? At the age of seven, I tried to comprehend events that had happened twenty years before. It was not a time I could touch but for some reason I felt it. And I had to know about it. I had to find a way to touch it.

During this time my family lived in Taiwan, where my father was stationed. As part of a welcoming ceremony the Taiwanese would place a string of firecrackers around one's house to chase away evil spirits and cleanse your house. Some friends of my parents decided to perform this ceremony for us but they failed to prepare us.

So one evening we were all at home having a quiet time when suddenly a horrible noise of extremely loud, rapid-fire cracks and bangs completely surrounded our house. I immediately panicked and began crying uncontrollably because I thought we had been found by soldiers, and machine-gun fire was going to murder my entire family. I didn't understand where I had heard this sound before or why I knew it signaled death; but at the age of seven all I could do was react. I could not explain to my family or myself why I was in such a panic. I was bewildered.

My neighborhood friends and I used to spend hours playing "army." We all had toy guns, and some of us even had uniforms of hats and shirts. I used to dream of getting an army outfit from the Sears catalog but I never did. We were all children of military families, so I guess it just seemed natural that we would play at war. It was actually great fun. We would break up into teams and try to capture the other team to win. The thrill of the chase while being chased was exhilarating!

But what was not easy for me to explain was that sometimes the game would go beyond the make-believe of a battle. After the battle when the enemy was caught, we would play games of interrogation and torture. Nothing physical ever occurred but we would fake whipping prisoners. And I recall that we all played both roles—the perpetrator and the victim. At the time, this was just part of our play. But I think now that a child's play can reveal a lot about children's feelings and identities.

As I got older and playing army was no longer something I did with my friends, I began to read books about World War II, anything I could get my hands on. I was especially fascinated by Leon Uris' *Exodus* and *QB VII*. They were stories about people, not just battles and dates. I was gripped by the personal aspect of the war.

I found myself studying German in high school and college because I thought it was interesting. The language came very easily to me; and I was able to read and pronounce the words quite naturally. I just thought it was easy for everyone. Studying German in college greatly stirred my desire to travel to Germany. But that was to come later.

.2.

In my late twenties I began to search for meaning in my life. I had been raised a Catholic but felt unfulfilled. I couldn't accept what others declared to be the truth; I had to find out for myself. I began to read books about reincarnation. This idea of living more than one life made more sense to me than just having one chance at it. I saw too much injustice and inequality in a world where everyone starts out with such different opportunities. However, I did believe in God and I didn't think that God would be so cruel that he wouldn't give everyone the same chance. There had to be more to this picture.

Also during this time I became involved in the first serious love relationship of my life. Because my lover was married, we both knew there was a definite limit to the relationship. We knew this going into it but decided it was worth it anyway. What I went through immediately following the breakup was the greatest challenge of my life to that point. When my lover left I was devastated. My heart was broken. I felt empty.

Existing from one day to the next was a challenge, and the meaning of it was nowhere to be found. Some days I didn't think I was going to make it through. I felt so drained. I forced myself to exercise. This was one way that I felt alive. If I felt pain in my muscles and my lungs, then at least I knew I was still alive. If you don't feel anything you're dead, right?

I thought about dying. But I thank God I didn't do anything to hurt myself. I finally sought out the help of a psychotherapist who assisted me through this difficult time, allowing me to move forward in my life.

But eventually the empty feeling dominated again. It never did go away, and then it began taking hold of my life. I felt purposeless. I couldn't see the point of life. I wasn't suicidal anymore but I was at the end of my road.

One morning I could not get out of my bed. I saw no point or purpose in getting up. A friend told me plainly as I lay there, "You need to see Pat. You need a soul retrieval." I hardly knew what soul retrieval was, but I knew immediately that she was right. Hearing truth in those words, I made plans to begin my inward journey of healing.

.3.

Pat was a friend of mine who practiced shamanism, a spiritual practice that has been used for healing in many cultures around the world for thousands of years. Pat had told me about the concept of soul loss and the technique of soul retrieval. I called her and we set up a time when I could visit. For the first time in a long time I felt hope about the future. I felt a new sense of energy. A couple of weeks later I went to see her.

The soul is the source of one's life force. It gives one the reason for living. But it is not a static structure. It is dynamic and responds to the occurrences of daily life, both the mundane and the dramatic. It is through the soul that one finds truth and the purpose of existence. But this is an ongoing process and not always easily revealed. Finding the truth of the soul is even more difficult when parts of the soul are missing. This is what had happened to me. Various traumas in my life had caused parts of my soul to leave me.

A person can lose a part of his or her soul when experiencing something perceived as very painful, whether it be physical or emotional. If the trauma is great enough a soul part must leave, taking the pain so that the person can survive. For a person to become whole, and therefore capable of fulfilling her destiny, she must reclaim these lost parts of her soul.

One way to retrieve lost soul parts is through shamanic soul retrieval. A shaman takes what is called a shamanic journey. By relaxing and listening to a steady drumming sound, the shaman is able to go into an altered state of consciousness. This allows the shaman's consciousness to travel outside of linear time and space into the world of spirit, nonordinary reality. Our normal waking state in the three-dimensional world is ordinary reality. But it is in nonordinary reality that lost soul parts are found.

My friend Pat had studied the shamanic technique of soul retrieval with Sandra Ingerman. She told me that before she would do my soul retrieval, she wanted to make sure that I had support of friends and my therapist. It was important for me to have that support, which I did.

Pat lived in an adjacent state, and it took me eight hours to drive to her house. This gave me time to reflect and prepare for the coming changes. Upon my arrival at her home, we began reviewing what we had discussed on the phone.

"So, tell me why you think you need a soul retrieval," she asked.

"I don't know where I am going with my life. I feel lost. I don't get it. Some days I just don't want to bother with getting out of bed. There doesn't seem to be any point."

"And you don't like this feeling?" she asked.

"No!" I insisted.

"You must realize that with soul retrieval there will be changes in your life," she explained. "When soul energy is returned you are no longer the same person. It will take time for you to adjust to the new you and for those around you to adjust. You have to ask yourself if you are willing to have change in your life. Part of the changes may involve the release of addictions that you have. A person may experience addictions because of the gaps left by soul loss. An addiction is the act of trying to fill the empty soul space with something that can never fill it. That is why addictions never end. Alcohol, drugs, and relationships can never make up for lost soul energy. Once the soul returns there is no room for the addiction. It may come down to either the soul part staying or the addiction staying. You must be prepared for this choice."

"I am ready for my life to change. I can't live like this any more," I assured her.

So Pat and I lay on a Navajo rug on the floor side by side, touching shoulder, hip and ankle. She played an unusual tape on her cassette stereo; it was the sound of rhythmic drumming. She then proceeded to journey into nonordinary reality in search of my lost soul. I lay there trying to stay calm and open. I was having doubts that she would find anything.

.4.

She returned from her journey holding her hands together in front of her heart. She sat up and leaned over me and gently blew my soul parts into my heart. I felt a rush of warmth and tingling. She helped me sit up and gently blew again into the top of my head.

The only way I can describe what I felt was that it was like pure love flowing into me. Tears of joy ran from my eyes. For the first time in my life I felt alive! It was weird, almost shocking to feel so much.

"Are you ready to hear about what I found?" she asked.

"Yes, but I'm already overwhelmed just by what I am feeling," I said.

She smiled. "I went with my spirit guides into nonordinary reality, asking for those soul parts that would be for your highest good to return at this time. The first part I came to was a small infant. Almost newborn. She was lying in her crib crying. I picked her up and comforted her for a while. I explained that I was here to bring her home. She stopped crying and I cradled her in my arms as I went looking for the next part.

"The second part I came to was a small child sitting on the ground open-legged playing jacks. I told her who I was, and that I was here to help her return to you. She was real easygoing and looked up and said 'okay.' And she told me that she had been waiting a long time. I took her by the hand and continued.

"The third part I came to was a little older. Perhaps ten years old. You were wearing a school uniform with a plaid skirt and white shirt. I repeated my purpose to her, but this child was angry and resistant. She said that you didn't want her back. So I talked to her for a while and assured her that you wanted her back, and after a while she agreed to come.

"I was then guided to a fourth part who looks as you do now. She was ready to return immediately and didn't say much.

"The fifth and last part I came across was unusual. It was a smattering of white particles floating in the air. There were many pieces. I was told this was another part of you. I found a glass vial and gathered all of the particles together into the bottle and put the lid on. Then I brought all the parts back to you."

I was amazed by how much of me had been out there. I didn't realize that so much had been missing. But in this moment I was feeling full and content. A peacefulness I had never known before came over me.

Now it was time for me to welcome my soul parts back home. I didn't know how to journey yet, so Pat suggested I meditate to meet with them.

She played some soothing music on the tape player and left the room. I was able to relax and meditate. I went to each part and spoke to them, welcoming them home and asking what they needed from me. The details that Pat had given me concerning how the parts looked impressed me. At the age of ten, I was in a Catholic school and we wore uniforms of a plaid skirt, white shirt and socks, and loafers, just as Pat had described. This was the year that my father was in Vietnam during the war there. He was stationed there for one year. His absence was very traumatic for me. Many nights I cried myself to sleep because I was sure he was never coming home again.

The adult part of me was lost when I broke up with my first real love, and it felt as if my heart had been ripped out. It was, in fact, this last piece that had pushed me over the edge into hopelessness.

The pieces of white fluff floating in the air were pieces of myself that I had given to physical therapy patients in the hope that it would help them. My first job as a physical therapist was in a large hospital, and I had spent a lot of time working in the ICUs dealing with people who were brain-injured and in comas. I wanted so much for these people to recover that I had offered my own soul to them. I know now that another person cannot make use of one's soul energy. But in my state of codependence I thought it might help. All it did was leave me more empty.

Until I had my soul retrieval I was really only going through the motions of life. It was as if I had been numb for the first thirty years of my life.

I thanked Pat and returned home the next day. After arriving home I spent the next several days thinking about all I had experienced. I found myself smiling a lot and just feeling happy to be alive. And the desire to understand all of this process and the reasons for the losses grew with each day.

I felt I understood the losses of all my parts except for the baby. It was at such an early age. I didn't think it had to do with this lifetime. It must have had something to do with the life previous to this. I had absolutely nothing to base this on. It was just a hunch, but I had always felt a deep sadness within me that was unexplainable. Something was missing, something that I couldn't quite put my finger on. It was something I knew but couldn't quite remember. I felt more and more that it had to do with a past life.

The need to know why the infant part of me had suffered sent me on the next leg of my journey. I had to know what had happened to me and was frustrated because there was nothing in my conscious memory from this time. The possibility of exploring past lives was very exciting to me, but how could I do it?

A friend told me about a woman who did channeling. I thought it might be a way to find out what happened if I simply asked her for the answer.

The channeler gave me interesting and valuable information, but it still wasn't enough. Something was missing. I felt a sadness deep within me that seemed to have no explanation. There was a key I needed to find—a key that I knew would unlock the past for me.

.5.

After some searching I found a therapist who did past life regressions. Her technique allowed me to stay conscious while going into an altered state and regressing in time. Throughout the session we talked to each other, and I tried to describe everything I was experiencing.

The theme of abandonment has occurred frequently in my life. We decided to start with the feeling of gut-wrenching pain that strikes my body when I perceive abandonment occurring. We traced this feeling back from adulthood to the very first time I could sense feeling it.

"Tell me what you are seeing," she asked as I lay in deep meditation.

"Well, I am in a room and it is kind of dark," I said, describing the scene in my head. "I can see a wall in front of me. The lighting in the room is very muted as if it is dusk or dawn—the time of day when it is neither truly light or truly dark."

"I'm feeling kind of panicky. I know someone was just here but they've left, and I don't know if they are coming back or not. I look down and I see a baby body. The stomach, hips, and little legs kicking in the air. Oh my goodness, this is my body! I'm not looking at the body, I'm in the body. I'm a baby! I try to get up but I can't. Someone just left and I have no idea if they're ever coming back again. Oh no!

"I'm on my back and I try to get up. Oh God, I can't even roll onto my side. I must be incredibly young. This is insane. My mind seems to know about getting up and walking but I can't make this body do it. I'm getting more panicky, and my arms and legs are scratching at the air trying to get me to move. I'm stuck!"

"It's okay. What do you do next?" she guides me.

"I'm freaking out. The more I try to move myself, the more I realize I can't and the more freaked-out I get. I can't help myself," I say, full of emotion.

"Oh my God, the pain. The pain is everywhere. Ohhh! But my gut. It's unbearable in my gut."

I begin to double over with the pain. And then everything goes dark. I can't see anything for a few moments. But the pain is still there. I become completely focused on my legs—bending and straightening them. Alternating. Right leg, left leg.

I'm bending my knees. Then straightening them out. Tightening every muscle as hard as I can. Right leg. Left leg. *Keep them moving. Must keep them moving.*

"I must keep them moving. I must keep them moving...or—"

"Or what?" she asks.

"I must keep them moving or else...or else...I...will...die! Oh God, I must keep them moving or else I will die! Oh my God, I'm dying. I don't want to die!" I exclaim.

"I'm on my back again but I'm not a baby anymore. My body is big. I'm an adult. And I'm on my back again. I'm on my back and I can't get up! Goddamn it! I can't get up! If I stop moving my legs, I know I'll die. Must keep them moving. But the pain. I can hardly bear the pain. As long as my legs are moving then I know I'm alive."

Slowly I start to realize that all around me is white. No buildings or trees. Just a huge expanse of whiteness. And it's cold. It's incredibly cold. The pain in my abdomen and legs is starting to spread throughout my entire body. It feels as if every single cell in my body is throbbing.

And then I realize I'm freezing to death, and there is nothing I can do to stop it. I'm on my back and I can't get up. But I keep resisting. I keep fighting. *Why am I so afraid to let go?*

And finally I hear my therapist say, "Yes, you have been abandoned. You were left to die alone."

With these words the wall of resistance fell within me, and I began to really cry. Feeling the sorrow of losing my life. Of losing my body. The fear of what will happen next. I was still so afraid to let go, but finally I felt a feeling of warmth encompass my being. And then there was an incredible white light and finally peace.

My body stopped shaking. The fear and sadness left. It was over.

I was, to say the least, blown away by this experience. Where had this come from? I had experienced death! My death!

As I drove home that night, the image of Siberia was extremely strong. In fact, it seemed to hit me at once. A voice in my head loudly exclaimed, "Siberia!" And I knew that this was the snowy landscape I was in. But when was this, and how had I ended up in such a desolate place?

.6.

For several days after this experience I was extremely emotional and cold. I released a lot of tears and sadness. An experience with a client triggered more sadness. She was an older woman who had had a stroke and was unable to sit by herself. I was working with her as she sat on a treatment table, and I had to hold onto her or she would fall over. She was completely helpless. She could not do anything for herself. Since my past-life regression I had become very familiar with the anguishing, inner pain of helplessness. It is consuming. I had to lay her back down on the mat and go into the bathroom and cry for a while. I cried for both her and myself.

It was amazing how strong all the feelings of my regression experience were. Each time I would tell the story to a friend, I could not get through it without crying or feeling cold. But each retelling began to feel like a healing. I knew this had to have been a past-life event but the impact of the emotions surrounding it blurred the boundary between lifetimes, and it felt as though it had happened yesterday.

One of the gifts of this experience was the sense that nothing in this life could be worse than knowing death. And knowing death has given me an edge on life, has taught me that the gift of life is precious and not to be taken lightly. Each day that is spent without awareness is a day lost.

Now I find myself puzzled by the people who are so concerned about living as long as possible. There are all kinds of books that discuss the secrets to extending life and I wonder why? For one thing, life is difficult and most people walk around in a fog, unconscious, and in great fear of death. Why would anyone want this to last any longer than it needs to?

It became clearer to me that the more energy people put into pushing death away, the more they are not really living. *Don't go there. Don't do that, you might die! Okay, I'll just stay here in this safe place and exist. It may be boring but at least I won't die!* When you embrace death, each moment of life is a miracle and is treasured, and you don't worry about tomorrow so much as you hold the preciousness of today in your being. There is no point in anger at the medical community for not finding cures to diseases fast enough. I have a sense that even as cures are found, new diseases arise because, as a group, the human race still does not understand the purpose of life and the purpose of dying. And so eradicating terminal illness would not serve us at this time.

But I saw that the notion of death as an end is an illusion. As I worked at unveiling my past, I discovered that my body has died many times but my soul seems continuous. Death is not the end; it never was.

The notion of living fully in each moment gave me inspiration the following day. I had a soccer game to play. The teams were evenly matched and it would be a tough game. On any given day, either team could win.

As the game started I was feeling emotional because of the regression. I expected to feel drained, and I thought I would have difficulty playing. To my surprise, and my teammates', I played with an intensity not normal for me. I always play hard but on this day I played as if there was no tomorrow.

I was going for the ball and confronting the other team as if I had nothing to lose. And I didn't. I already knew what it was like to die. I knew that I could play as hard as I wanted and I wouldn't die. It's fear that keeps me from achieving sometimes. I wasn't afraid anymore.

One particular moment stands out in my memory. The ball had gone out-of-bounds and I ran after it. There were no spectators on this side of the field, and my back was to the other players. I seemed alone in this moment, and the emotional release that began the day before wanted to reoccur right then. I slowed my run to a walk and took a few deep breaths before picking up the ball. I said to myself, "No, I am not going to cry." I turned around and went back on the field determined not to be sad. As I threw the ball back into play I actually felt an increase in energy. Instead of feeling sad and crying, I turned the energy that was asking for release into enthusiasm for playing. I played the game with all I could give on that day. Winning or losing seemed unimportant. It was the joy at being part of the play and giving my all that was fulfilling.

Oh, as an aside, we did win the game. I didn't say that I had *completely* forgotten about winning and losing!

.7.

The experience of this first past-life regression sparked an intense need within me to know it all. I was very curious to know if this event of the death in the snow was the last life and what had led up to it. So I continued.

In the next session I was guided specifically into the life previous to my current one. I found myself standing on a hill overlooking a burning city. The air is thick with yellow smoke as the sun tries to filter through. It's late afternoon and the sun is low in the western sky. Billowy columns of black smoke rise up from all around the city. There is a stench in the air. I realize I am looking at a city that has just been bombed.

I look down my body and I see I have on black leather boots, and brown woolen pants and jacket. I am wearing a hat with a brim in the front, sort of like a baseball cap but not really. It feels as if it's made of wool also.

I'm very distraught. I want to go back into the city. I sense that my family is there. I want to save them but I also know that I need to run from the city or I will be caught. I feel so torn, not able to move in either direction. I hear a voice say, "So what do you do?" I run. I run as fast and as hard as I can away from the city. I head east. I know there is nothing I can do for my family. I'm not even sure if they are alive anymore. For whatever reason I must save myself.

In the next scene I find myself in a barren, hilly area with thousands of men and women. Some are hitting the hard, rocky ground with pick-axes, and others are carrying the dirt away in baskets. Armed guards are scattered throughout the area. I have a pick-axe in my hand and I'm striking the earth. I feel the power and strength of my shoulders and arms and realize I'm a man. What a difference there is between a man's body and a woman's. Part of me wishes I could have that kind of strength in this life.

A fence surrounds the entire area. I am a prisoner. It must be a labor camp. This must be Siberia! An incredibly hopeless feeling comes up: *I am never going to get out of here.* The people here all look lifeless, empty. Their souls are gone. Their bodies are going through movements with no feeling of purpose or reason.

I look down at my clothes and see they are torn and shredded. I still have my boots. It must be summer because there is no snow around.

The scene fades and now I find myself in midwinter, marching in snow in a line of men. We are all tied together by a rope. My hands are bound together in front of me, as are everyone else's. We are in the middle of nowhere and are being forced to march with no apparent destination or purpose. But I soon realize there is a one-and-only-purpose, to be marched until we die.

The man in front of me falls, and I help him back up. They beat me with sticks for helping him. They cut him out of the rope, and we are forced to continue on. I hear a gunshot behind me.

It seems that we are walking forever, with the guards beating us all the time. My face feels very puffy and swollen. My whole body feels broken. I have fallen several times but always I get back up. I fall once more but this time I can't get up. The guards are kicking and beating me, yelling at me to get up. I can't. My legs are broken. Oh, the pain! I can't move. My entire body is numb with pain. They cut the rope and leave me lying in the snow. I can see them marching away toward the horizon. They have left me to die. Not even the compassion of a bullet to shorten my suffering.

At this point I recall my first regression and see that this is what led up to the death I had seen. Not needing or wishing to reexperience the moments before death, I move forward to the point of death. I rise above my body and see it lying in the snow. It looks very emaciated, as if I had aged forty years in a very short time. My sense for the period of time was the late 1940s or early 1950s.

My therapist called me back. The regression ended. Now I knew how I had gotten into the situation of dying in the snow. Now I knew why I couldn't get up and why I had died alone. But I was still confused about how I had become a labor camp prisoner and what city I had been running away from. My strong sense was that it was eastern Europe.

A short time after this second regression I had another soul retrieval. Pat found a part of me next to my body in the snow. I looked like the man I had been in the last life. He had felt guilt and that he didn't deserve to move forward. It had something to do with having had to leave his family in the burning city.

.8.

Following the soul retrieval I listened to a tape about forgiveness and self-love, called "Igniting the Spark." It said you cannot love others until you love yourself first, and the key to loving yourself is forgiving yourself. This was new to me; although I had known that part of loving others was to include forgiveness, I had never applied this concept to myself. I was always hardest on myself.

Anyway, there was a meditation on forgiving yourself for something you had done in the past that you felt was unforgivable. Well, I went along with this and thought about something I had done in my childhood that I could forgive myself for. I began visualizing myself as a child and sending love and forgiveness. But what happened next amazed me because the child left, and the part of me that was left in the snow appeared. I saw this man in tattered clothes, disheveled, standing before me and asking forgiveness. I was overwhelmed with emotion.

He felt unforgivable because he had lived while his family had died. He/I felt he/I had abandoned his/my family. I embraced this part of myself and told him that, yes, he was forgiven. And that I was sorry it had taken me so long to do this. He was very understanding. I felt so much love for myself. I had never known that the joyful, loving way I have embraced others in my life, I could also extend to myself. And how full I felt!

I realized that my life patterns are clues about what is asking to be healed. I found that the pattern of abandonment wasn't about me having been abandoned but about the guilt I carried for having to leave my family in the burning city. Each time I felt abandoned in this life was an opportunity to forgive myself. Once I did, I felt I would never have that feeling of abandonment again. And I haven't.

.9.

Approximately six weeks after my first past-life regression I took a trip to what was then West Berlin, West Germany, to attend a workshop. Little did I know what was to occur.

I was very excited about this trip. I had always wanted to go to Europe and finally see the Germany I had studied for so many years. Stepping off the plane on a warm June afternoon and feeling the air of West Berlin, I had a sense of familiarity. I was very happy to be there. Walking around the streets filled me with joy. I thought I was just excited to be in a foreign country. I love to travel.

This was in June 1989. The Berlin Wall was still in existence, and communism seemingly maintained a strong hold on eastern Europe. One day while going for a run, an image flashed through my mind of me being in Berlin as a child. I quickly rejected this thought, clearly stating to myself that I had never been in Berlin before so I couldn't possibly have been here as a child. But I was to find that each day I spent in Berlin provided more and more evidence to me of a prior existence there.

One day my companions and I took a trip into East Berlin. It was mind-boggling. As soon as I entered the eastern sector I could feel a distinct difference from the west. There was a heaviness in the air. People didn't look you in the eye, and they all seemed sad. I don't remember any smiling faces in East Berlin.

The main boulevard in this part of the city is the Unter Den Linden. It is an attractive street with grand buildings. But my companions and I decided to venture off the beaten path, and we veered away from the Unter den Linden. What I saw on the side streets amazed me. Bombed out, lifeless buildings had been left unrepaired since the war. Their skeletal remains had walls with no roofs and the remnant of a storied floor here and there. Glass from the windows was long gone. Only the rubble that must have been in mounds around the bases of the buildings had been removed. And everywhere were the pockmarks from bullets.

I couldn't believe what I was seeing after forty-four years. It felt as though it was still 1945! I could still hear the pinging of bullets ricocheting off the concrete and bombs flying through the air and crashing into buildings and people. My consciousness altered with all that I saw and felt. Such deep sadness was there. I felt myself asking, *why did this have to happen?*

I walked around these stone corpses, transported back in time. I heard a voice inside of me say that on this street I should see....and the name of someone I thought I should know attempted to come to consciousness like a word just on the tip of my tongue. There was the feeling of a familiar face that I should see when I round this corner. Who?! Where did that come from? I began to dialogue with myself. One part was totally comfortable with where I was, even familiar with the streets and the people that should be living there. Another voice was saying, "*Are you crazy? How can you possibly know people in a place you have never been before?*"

But a part of me knew this place—knew these streets.

My companions had to keep calling me to stay up with them. I was walking slower and slower, trying to take everything in. Trying to understand. I could hear echoes of familiar voices speaking in a foreign tongue. I could see shadows of familiar people for an instant, and then they were gone. Mentally I was struggling with these incomprehensible occurrences. It didn't seem to be happening to anyone else I was with. What was going on with me? I felt as though the buildings were talking to me.

I also sensed the pain and the hiding of the current residents that day. The joylessness. People were living in buildings that had bullet-ridden exteriors. How awful to live with daily reminders of a time long ago that was full of pain and loss.

We only spent a few hours of an afternoon exploring East Berlin but for me it felt like a lifetime. I didn't want to leave. Going back to the west was like entering another world. The separateness and division that the wall was able to create was overwhelming. The burden this land carried was enormous.

In the train station that processed everyone going east and west there was an interesting mixture of people. There were young West Germans of school age who had spent an afternoon in the east as part of a school trip. They were laughing and having fun with each other, seemingly unaware of the heaviness around them. Then there were the older people who lived in the east and were returning home after some time in the west. East Germans over a certain age were allowed to travel to the west, but their faces were empty, tired, burdened. They were prisoners returning to their cells. The pain I felt from them seemed incurable. It was rather a schizophrenic atmosphere.

And I was rather schizophrenic myself, in the sense that throughout my stay in Berlin I was very happy and very sad, mostly at the same time. I was at home and in a foreign country at the same time. But through it all I was intrigued and wanted to know where all these feelings were coming from.

The last day I was in Berlin the sun rose on a brilliant and peaceful Sunday morning. I got up early and went for a run. I looked at a map and decided on a route that would take me to the Brandenburg Gate and the Berlin Wall at the center of the divided city.

This early morning run was wonderful; the streets were deserted. I felt I had the city to myself. I turned east onto the broad boulevard called Bismarckstrasse. The sun was rising and its warmth reassured me that I was headed in the right direction. I was three miles from the wall.

I ran past grand university buildings and monuments. Still the reminders of the war were ever-present. In the west the repairs had been completed but one could tell what had been damaged. And that was just about everything! Everywhere the old and the new were melded together. Every block of buildings and houses was interspersed with prewar and postwar construction. Within individual buildings an old wall would round a corner and meet a new one. The physical evidence of the war aided in altering my state of consciousness, and with each step I went deeper. Soon I felt as if bullets were whizzing by my head. Bombs were exploding all around me, and my body reacted by sidestepping, attempting to dodge the explosions. My eyes told me that everything was peaceful and calm, but my inner experience was very different.

I left the buildings and entered the tree-lined Tiergarten. I felt a welling of intense emotion in my abdomen. With each stride it grew. I didn't understand what this was but I was beyond discussion or choice in the matter. I was driven to reach the wall. The emotion in my abdomen gradually became recognizable as overwhelming sadness.

About a mile from the wall I started to hyperventilate and had to stop running for a moment. I wanted to cry and didn't know why. I forced myself to breathe deeply and calm down enough so that I could run again. I had to get to the Wall.

Within a hundred yards of the wall the emotion in my gut overwhelmed me and I started to cry. I had never felt so much sadness in my life. I found myself staring at the wall, and I heard myself say, "What have they done to my city?!" The pain I felt was as if my heart had been ripped open.

I knew at once that my spiritual eyes had seen this city before. I had known the beauty of Berlin. But now for the first time I saw it divided. I knew that the last time I had seen Berlin, it was whole. I was shaken by this revelation. I just sat and stared at the wall in disbelief. How did this happen? Again

I felt the ghosts of Berlin as I had felt them in the east. It seemed that they were calling me.

.10.

I was sad to leave Berlin but also relieved. So much had come to me that I felt I couldn't handle any more. But I left without a doubt I would be back.

After I got back home I could tell I had changed. My ideas about the limitations of human existence and who I was had grown tenfold. Everything seemed bigger, and life had many more possibilities than I had ever before imagined. The essence of who I was knew more than this lifetime of experience. To me this was very exciting.

One of the many experiences of Berlin that left its mark on me was meeting a young West German woman from Cologne named Paula. We met on the first day of the conference I had attended. We found that we had similar professional interests, and we discussed these over lunch. We agreed to meet again and talk more. As we parted that day I watched her walk away, and a bell went off in my head. It was a ringing like a school bell but not very loud. At the time I had no idea what this meant, but the image of her walking away and the bell going off are indelibly printed in my memory. I know now that this bell in my head is a signal of recognition, and it is especially strong when I reunite with someone from the last life. I have experienced it several times since.

The day after I had the incredible experience in East Berlin, I talked with Paula. Initially we talked about the conference and our jobs, then I began to tell her how I couldn't believe the disrepair of East Berlin from the war. With very little reaction or concern, she responded that if I thought East Berlin was bad, I should see the other cities in the east. They were worse. East Berlin was the pride of East Germany and was given the most attention!

I was amazed at this but in another sense was not surprised since I had been conditioned to think not very highly of the Communist system and its efficiency. She also told me that no city in Germany was untouched by the war in the final days. I realized that, as an American, I had no real concept of the destruction of war.

Paula also told me that she didn't really care about the east because for her it was a separate country. She was born after the war and had never known Germany whole. Her thinking surprised me because in my mind both East and West Germany made up the whole. They were separated by political systems but to me they were one people. She had no desire for reunification. And in June 1989, she, like many other Germans, didn't think it possible.

At any rate, I still needed to connect with this German woman on a deeper level. Taking a chance, I asked her if she ever had the feeling that she had lived somewhere before. She paused and looked at me quizzically and then said, "You mean like in another life?" Amazed at how quickly she picked up on what I was trying to say, I responded happily "Yes!" I told her that I knew I had lived in eastern Europe before because of the past-life regressions. I went on to tell her of my experience in East Berlin.

As I talked I felt myself lift up out of my body, and I observed Paula and myself from overhead. For me, time had stopped. We connected on a verbal level, but so much more was happening on other levels also. She was fascinated with what I said but also confused. She had heard about reincarnation but never had any direct experience. I guessed she didn't really know what to think of this American she had just met. But whatever happened between us was very strong, and we both wanted to maintain a relationship. We exchanged addresses and phone numbers and promised to keep in contact.

After my first few days home I wanted to write Paula but was afraid. All that had happened to me was incredible; having a connection with a living person in Germany made the reality too close. But it was clear that I really didn't have a choice. I had to keep in contact with her. We communicated frequently in the coming months through letters and the phone. Neither one of us really understood what was going on between us but we were compelled to find out. She came to America to visit me over the next Christmas.

In the meantime I continued my search for answers to why this experience in Berlin had happened and what it meant for me now. I went for another channeling.

.11.

As with all the channelings, it was tape-recorded. The information I received jarred me. I found out that I indeed had been German and had lived in Berlin with my family during the time of the Nazis.

As the words were spoken in the channeling, this image and event began to play out for me. It was like watching a movie. No, it was like being in the movie and experiencing all of the events first-hand, as well as all the emotion within myself.

I am crouched down in the basement of my house peering out a musty, dirty window. There has been a great commotion outside. Soldiers are all around. Orders are being shouted. There is a loud bang as the front door is thrown open. I hear screams and yelling from inside my house. They are my mother's anguished cries as my father is dragged outside. He is being beaten. My sister is huddled against me. It's all happening so fast. Two helmeted soldiers come down the stairs with machine guns in their hands. They grab my sister from me. She is screaming and crying for me to save her. They pull her out of my arms. They look at me strangely and leave, dragging my sister with them.

I hear a gun shot and turn to look out the window just as my father's body crumples in a heap to the ground. The soldiers have ripped the clothes off of my mother and sister and are on them, beating and raping them to death. I don't know how much time has gone by. My house is in shambles. My family is dead. In a matter of moments my whole world is gone.

The channeling continued:

> "*And you were slippery and able to escape. And the guilt of having observed your family being abused and killed and your propensity for being slippery and evasive has heavily programmed you with guilt with regard to abandonment. You could not justify that you had lived and they had died. It wore heavily upon your heart.*
>
> "*And eventually, by your early thirties, you literally died of a broken heart, unable to sustain the guilt any longer.*
>
> "*Through the physical situation you have remembered in regard to the prison camp situation and your freezing in Siberia, the actual creation of termination of life on a personal choice level was that you no longer had the heart to live. You no longer had the will to go on. This residual energy is the energy you experience in this lifetime, which you label as being nonmotivated, lethargic, or lazy, when in actuality you are a very energized and action-oriented being. And this counterpart of self occurs infrequently though devastatingly when it is felt, as it reminds you of this time when your life force was so diminished that literally the spark of life left you. And the experience was chilling, was freezing, was being left cold.*"

I was stunned. I felt the impact of the truth of these words to my core. The flood of emotion felt endless. In a matter of a few moments, I finally understood the source of the deep grief and sadness I had carried with me all my life. My whole family was gone. And here in 1989 I felt the loss as if it had just happened. The intellectual knowledge that my current family was alive and well did nothing to console me. In this moment I had only one family and they were gone. Torn out of my arms. Murdered before my own eyes.

And now I know that the burning city had been Berlin. I knew the streets of East Berlin because I had lived there before. After witnessing my family's murder I had run from the city.

Taking in a deep breath and closing my eyes once again, I find myself standing on a hilltop. Exhausted and breathless I gaze in disbelief at the burning and smoking ruins of the city that used to be my home. Once majestic buildings stand roofless and defeated. Mountains of concrete and bricks fill what were once bustling streets. The streets have been swallowed up by rubble as far as the eye can see. The sky is filled with black and brown smoke. The sunlight low in the western sky is filtering through the pall of death and destruction. Just enough light remains to make one think there is still hope. But the stench of rotting bodies buried in the rubble almost palpably awakens one to the reality of hopelessness. The dead and dying walk the streets. Some no longer inhabit bodies. They are forever sentenced to haunt the defeated city. I can feel them.

Memories of my life flash before my eyes. All that I knew and loved is gone. My heart is heavy with grief and despair. Hoping in desperation that maybe it has all been a bad dream, I imagine going home. My mother and father will be there to greet me as always—Mom in the kitchen baking and Pop in his favorite chair reading the evening paper. But I hear a voice telling me I must turn and run. But...my family. And insistently I hear, "You must go now. They are no more. It is over for them. For you there is more. Leave. Leave now!" Hesitatingly I turn and run.

I run east. I run and run as if literally trying to run away from myself. With tears in my eyes and sorrow in my heart, I am no longer sure of who I am or where I am. I see bombs flying over my head. I hear them explode somewhere behind me. I don't look.

Climbing over and through broken buildings, I pass people scampering like rats among the rubble, fighting over scraps of bread, no longer human. I pass through a park that was once splendid and green, filled with happy, laughing children playing tag among green-leafed giants, now standing as blackened, amputated tree trunks. The children are long gone. Many are buried in the snows of the east.

Bodies hang from street lamps. A sign around the neck of a boy no more than fifteen years old says, "Verräter." Traitor. The sentence of accused deserters. How can one desert a catastrophe?

There is nothing to fight for anymore. I struggle to recall if there ever was anything to fight for. My mind is confused and blurred.

Opening my eyes now, I take in another deep breath. Soberly I acknowledge to myself this was World War II and I was German. A German male.

I began to fit the pieces together with the history I knew of the time. Knowing that it was soldiers who murdered my family, I felt that it must have been the Russians. The battle for Berlin was won by the Russian army, and no German was safe. Irrationally I ran east from the city, right into the arms of the Russian army. I was captured and finally ended up in Siberia. "Left cold."

My immediate sense of recognition of Paula was made clearer; she was someone I had known in the labor camp. We were both prisoners and had given each other support. In the camp we were not allowed to speak, and we communicated on a telepathic level. This was why so much more was happening between us when we talked in Berlin. We were connecting on levels deeper than speech allows.

For several days following this channeling I existed in an altered state. It was a struggle to remind myself what year it actually was. I would be walking around town and talking to people but I was in a mist. It was like a dream. The delineation of time was a blur. The sense of loss and the guilt of surviving dominated. I cried for days.

.12.

The next few months were filled with discoveries about Paula's and my relationship and what it offered each of us. We were both intrigued and excited. Hearing her German accent over the phone altered me in time and space. It was incredible to have a relationship with this person. I was very excited to have a connection with someone living in Germany. Through Paula, Germany became alive and present for me. It wasn't just a place on a map or in history books. The war had not been a fantasy nor had my remembering been an illusion.

I was fascinated by the idea that fifty years ago I had been German, speaking another language. I was even a different sex! I wondered if this recent time as a male was perhaps why I had been such a tomboy growing up in this life. I don't know, but it certainly seemed to make some sense. At any rate, I began to look at *who am I really? Who am I if, not so long ago, I was of another nationality, another culture that to me now seems foreign?*

Paula and I talked about this, and she told me how she had inklings all her life that she had been Jewish before. But she had never told anyone because she was afraid to admit this. Even today people in Germany are still hesitant to talk about being Jewish. This amazed me because I had thought this was no longer an issue. But then I was to find that I knew very little about Germany and what it is like to live there now.

During this time I began to struggle with the conditioned feelings I have had all my life that Germans are bad, that they had done this terrible thing a long time ago. Things that "we Americans" would never have done or allowed to happen. I can remember in comic books that the bad guys were usually Nazis, and they would do terrible things to the good guys. And now I was finding that I was on the other side. I had been on the side that had been bad. But now I was on the good side. Now I was on the side that had saved the world! So what does it all mean? Who am I?

I am American. I was German. I am both. I am neither. This thinking planted in me the idea that nationalities mean nothing because probably we have all been each other—not in the sense of our core selves or soul but in the outer physical trappings we wear of race and nationality. There is no place on the planet that I cannot imagine having lived.

Perhaps conflicts between nations are just mirroring conflicts within ourselves. I have been German, and possibly Chinese or African or Russian, as there is a part of myself that can identify with each one. And if, as an American, I fight a Russian and I have been Russian, then there is the sense that I am actually fighting an aspect of myself. And this kind of conflict begins to seem really crazy.

I began to sense how I am me and the whole at the same time. Separating myself from the whole would be like saying I am only the heart within a human being and that is all. But a heart cannot survive without the whole being. And the being cannot survive without the heart.

So much separation is created by nationalism and racism, which in a way creates separation in our individual souls. The idea that we are different and separate is an illusion. Healing will come only through union. Separation is death.

.13.

This idea became more clear to me in a journey some time later. I had taken a course in shamanic journeying and began to use this technique as a way to travel back into the German lifetime. Using the shamanic journey to get information, was empowering. Instead of asking someone else for information, I was able to make direct contact with my spiritual guides.

I access nonordinary reality by visualizing an opening in the earth, like a hole in the ground, a tree, a cave, or a body of water. I often use a very special place in nature that I have visited in ordinary reality. When I am ready to journey I find a comfortable place to lie down in my house; often it will be in my bedroom. I place a covering over my eyes so that any light in the room will not distract me. I listen to the steady drumming through a pair of headphones.

After a few moments of drumming I see myself standing at my place in nature, and I then enter the earth. Immediately I am in a tunnel that I travel down. I see the light at the end of the tunnel, and when I come out into the light I am in what is called the Lower World. It is here that I meet with my many guides that are in animal form. They are called power animals, and I see mine as a kind of guardian angel. I have the sense that they are with me always, whether or not I am journeying.

I talk to my power animal and tell him the purpose of my journey. Sometimes we talk for a while, or he shows me scenes that relate to my question. Anything can happen in a journey; answers may be verbal or symbolic, in the form of images or just a feeling with no visual effect. Information can be relayed any number of ways in this altered state.

The end of the journey is signaled by a change in the rhythm of the drumming. This tells me to retrace my steps back to the place where I entered the earth and go back to ordinary reality.

In this journey I asked about the purpose of nationalities and all the differences we seem to create between ourselves. I was shown a scene from the eastern front during the war. There were rows of Germans dug into the snow on one side. And facing them only a few hundred yards away were rows of Russian soldiers in their trenches. It was trench warfare just as in World War I.

I found myself immersed in the chaos of the battle. Bullets were flying all around. Friends have fallen, and there is blood in the snow. But then the sounds of the battle fade away. I hear a voice telling me to look closely at the Russian soldiers. Look closely. I rise above the battle and look down at both sides clawing and screaming to kill so as to not be killed. The voice says, "Look closely at the faces. They are not different. They were once German. And many of your German comrades were once Russian. Look at how they have traded sides. Look at how they play at the same game but from different sides of the board. In the last great war (WWI) many on each side wore the uniform of their current enemy. They think this is the first time. It is simply the most recent of many, many episodes. They don't remember. And because of this they are doomed to repeat this scene over and over until they remember. I am telling you this because you must remember. It must stop."

So there were Russians who just twenty-five or so years prior had been German and vice versa. And I couldn't help but think, *how many times do we have to kill ourselves before we get it, that killing is not the answer?*

.14.

But as for Paula and me, the more we talked with each other, the more we both began to see that we shared a core connection, and that differences in language and upbringing—the outer coverings of who we appeared to be—did not matter. What we found for each other was love.

During this time I was slowly putting together the series of events of my last life. Assuming that it was the Russians who murdered my family, I didn't understand why I had been allowed to escape. It must have been near the end of the war when Berlin was being destroyed and overrun. I began to read any account of the war—and especially about Berlin—that I could get my hands on, most importantly anything written from the German perspective. I was so tired of hearing about how the Americans had defeated Nazism, and that the Germans were inhuman, cold. I didn't believe this. As an American I knew very little of the German side of things, but I was determined to find out. Because now I knew that I have been both American and German. Germans must not be all bad!

.15.

In the months following my trip I began to have dreams of Germany and the war. The dreams were mostly bits and pieces of scenes. In one, I had been in a building that was being bombed and I barely escaped. And I remember feeling guilt at not being able to help anyone else get out. People were buried in the rubble.

In other dreams, all I remembered upon waking was having had a close brush with death. In one I escaped a ship that was sinking; in another I was in full retreat as bullets were flying all around me.

I would dream of my German family. I saw myself as a child walking down cobblestone streets holding my father's hand. My father was a young man, and I felt very safe and secure with him. I was five years old and the year was 1926. I had shoes with little buckles on them and a jacket and shorts like a little sailor's suit. And I remember how I had a little blue sailor shirt with a white tie in this life and how much I loved that shirt. Maybe that was because it reminded me of another time when I was happy.

And then the scene shifted to 1933. I was 12 years old. Everyone in Germany was happy. We were proud to be Germans. My father fought in World War I, and he said that there should never be another war. I saw my parents as very loving towards each other. My mother was beautiful. And my sister annoyed me but I loved her.

I would wake up yearning for this family and still feeling the loss. As the survivor, I felt responsible to do something about them. I had asked in a journey if they were present on the planet now, and I kept getting the answer that they weren't, or at least that I shouldn't get obsessed with trying to find them—which would have been easy to allow myself to do, since I felt such a longing for them.

A few months later I had another dream of seeing my parents as a young couple very much in love. They were not my current parents, and it became clear to me they were my German parents. We were at a restaurant and I went to get the car to take them home. When I returned with the car they were gone. I spent the rest of the dream searching for them but I never found them.

When I woke up, the feeling of searching for my family and needing to return to Germany was very strong.

Every day my thoughts were of that lifetime and of Germany. Feeling very driven to want to know more. I think that the people around me got a little tired of this "obsession." I knew that they didn't quite understand what it was that was driving me, and I often felt pressure not to take it so seriously or to drop it, but I couldn't. I was driven by something beyond me.

Any movie or book that had anything remotely to do with Berlin or the war I would watch or read. I couldn't get enough.

.16.

Intermixed with the events of the past was the dilemma of patterns that were troubling my current life. Anger was a problem. I would overreact to some situations, and often these situations would have something to do with men.

I wasn't even aware that I had a dislike toward men until my early twenties while I was still in Hawaii paddling outrigger canoes for a racing club. These clubs had a mixture of men, women, and kids. I don't remember exactly how it came up, but when one of my female friends was talking with a group of the men, they commented that they knew that I didn't like men. I was shocked at this information. I didn't see myself like that. Yet these men who hardly knew me had picked up on it.

I thought about it. Every time I was in a situation where I perceived that a man was trying to manipulate a woman, I would get very angry. And then I received more information in a channeling regarding this, which helped to clarify the source of my anger.

"And in respect to your extreme aversions to the male gender of your race, this past life has much to do with it. For in your consciousness the pillaging and the rape, the abuse, the nonrecognition of mankind within form was primarily professed and utilized by the male gender. And you hold a very strong and great resentment that their consciousness was so dense that they would participate in such dense activity.

"You are holding that strain. You are holding that cord. And letting go will assist you in an equality in consciousness, though *it will not change anything in reference to your preference. It will allow a release of the anger and hostility that has held. Forgive, forgive, forgive them, for they know not what they do. And this is in truth the case as it may be. For those who carry a denser form of energy are less available for antennas of light."*

How was I going to be able to forgive this? I did have anger toward men. And now I knew that carrying this density was blocking me. Holding on to hatred and anger clearly did not serve me. And maintaining it by directing it outward would never heal it. It wouldn't be until I could own this within myself that I would heal. Men were only mirroring to me my self-hatred of my own maleness. And I hated them even more for constantly reminding me of my own dark past.

.17.

This idea of forgiveness would have to be taken much further than forgiveness for another. Strangely I was able to forgive Hitler before I was able to forgive myself.

The words of this next channeling would continue to echo in my consciousness for the next several years. They would often give me strength when I would doubt or feel weak from the enormity of it all. The keys about forgiveness and control would be paramount to my healing. And the words to this day reverberate in my mind. . . .

"You have most definitely been a young man living in Berlin in your most recent past lifetime. You have experienced the trauma of seeing those you loved annihilated, abused, the land being bludgeoned, and the environment going from health and community to fear and oppression. You have seen members of your family literally ripped from your arms. And there are scars that need healing.

"And you have returned to heal these scars. And the greatest healer is to forgive. For please do remember, Maryanne, that it is an illusion: that it is a drama, a play, and that it is no more real than the passing thoughts that change from moment to moment within you. And it was a reality. And that is the duality of this consciousness. For it is hard to understand how the drama can be so physically felt if it is only a play.

"It is by choice that you, mankind, have come into physical form to experience the sensations that cause growth. It is by choice that oftentimes those sensational realizations are dramatic and hostile. For much is learned in fear and contraction. It is such an extreme state of resistance that each individual tries to remove themselves from this limited state of consciousness as quickly as possible.

"And hence, a time is coming when there is choice. And the choice will be to experience growth without the necessity of it being so painful, so archaic, so unenlightened. And yet many are stuck in believing that the only way to experience life is through the density of the thickened emotional body.

"And not only that—they crave these excitations, these experiences, to journal them, to verbalize them, to resist them. They are always doing something with them rather than allowing them to pass, knowing that it is changing, changing, changing.

"And each individual is in the mode of change, expansion, and contraction, creating the momentum of change experienced on a cellular level at a subatomic rate. This changing life force is occurring perpetually, continually.

"And yet you, mankind, choose to believe that you can hold onto the moment, can hold onto all that is good and you will be safe. And the letting go is what is necessary. A letting go of all the control of trying to make it the way it is not, rather than accepting the way that it is.

"And hence, you have returned to Berlin to remind you that what you have experienced is real. And that that experience has made an impact on you in your cellular body. And what you truly returned to Berlin to do was to clear, to purify, to release that emotional impact into the hollowness of what exists there now. For what is there to hold onto? For what was is no longer. Let it go. And in this you will experience great freedom in your spirit.

"And for those who have chosen to situate themselves there (East Berlin) and live the life of constraint, to live within the confines of oppressive law and theory—let them have their experience. Empower them with the knowingness that they have chosen their reality, and that they are not victimized by it, and that they are learning from it, and that it is their own natural course. And release them to suffer as they will or to flower as they might.

"These are the connections. The solution is universal love. The solution is alchemically to take denser matter and to fill it with light and to create lighter matter.

"And this you must do in your emotional body in regard to the devastation of your country, of your city, of your ideology, of the essence of freedom within yourself. And this freedom must come from within. And this love from within. And this forgiveness from within. And this disillusion of the density dissolving from within.

"Part of this process for you is totally immersing yourself into the materials of the time. Historical remembering. Moving through it and coming out in the light. Your chosen plan.

"So near to you was this last life that it is really impressed upon your beingness. You have specifically chosen to return in this life to clear that energy effectively and efficiently from self, as you cannot proceed in your purpose in your light work carrying the trauma and hatred that you have carried through into this life as a residual matter from another.

"And when you look back and see what is the purpose, what a huge perception crosses your mind. For what is the purpose of war? What is the purpose of abandonment of human spirit, of debasing the human spirit? What is the purpose of all of this? And in the center, in the truth, in light of what is, it is control.

"The purpose of war is control. To control another country. To control another spirit. To be in charge and separate from.

"And the lesson you have learned and have the potential to learn in this life is that control is not the answer. For in truth, you are in control when you are out of control. If you will reflect upon athletic experience—you run best when you are not considering how you are running. The energy is flowing through you or moving and being propelled by something beyond your own thoughts. This is truly the ultimate flow.

"And the ultimate flow creates the ultimate precision of movement. The ultimate precision of spirit and the ultimate, if you will, control. This is when you make no errors. This is when you make no mistakes. This is when you are simply feeling, moving, being with what is."

Releasing control would become my greatest challenge, and it would take me years. It doesn't happen all at once. You release a little and then another challenge arises that takes you to a deeper level of release. One thing I have discovered with my inner work and healing is that the lessons and challenges always get harder. Just when I think I have arrived, the next challenge appears, and it always seems just a little too much for me. But with time and patience—and some resistance and denial—I eventually do move through, although I do tend to kick and scream at times.

.18.

In the midst of these revelations and insights the Berlin Wall came down. The wall fell November 9, 1989. While the physical structure was coming down in Berlin, walls of another nature were coming down within my own soul, revealing more of my German lifetime and my being.

I came home from work that evening and turned the television on to see a mass of joyous people standing on top of and around the wall drinking champagne and partying. It was incredible to see people feel so free in an area that previously meant certain death. I felt such joy to see East and West Germans celebrating together. It was as if my mother and father had gotten back together after a lengthy separation. I was mesmerized as I sat and watched the people in their exhilaration and joy.

And on a deeper level I felt that finally the war was over. Finally, the healing could begin. I realized that as long as the wall was present, the massive wound it attempted to cover—the wound of Fascism—would never heal. The wall had only created the illusion that the trauma of the war was over.

I meditated that night and gave thanks to all who assisted in creating the fall of the wall. As I did, I found myself transported to Berlin. I was among the cheering, jubilant crowd. I had a pick-axe in my hands and was hammering away at the wall. It was an incredible feeling of power to be literally knocking the wall down.

After a few moments I heard someone call my name. I turned around and saw my German mother, father, and sister. And I realized as soon as I saw them that they hadn't called me by "Maryanne" but by "Hans". And I responded as naturally to Hans as I would to Maryanne. We were all crying tears of joy. We were finally reunited.

I looked down at my body and saw that I looked as I did in the last life. But what I noticed now that was disturbing was that I realized I was wearing a soldier's uniform. It was the uniform of a German soldier and it was mine. This was something I did not want—as if I could change what has already occurred years before. I was willing to accept that I had been German and a male but had hopes I had been a civilian, and not directly involved in the devastation of Europe. Now I knew that things had not been the way I desired them to be.

The weight of this information brought much sadness to me. Somehow I knew that these hands holding a pick-axe, chopping away for freedom, had killed many people. The guilt made the axe feel very heavy. But in the same moment I was also re- lieved—since I would rather deal with the truth of the situation than a fantasy—that this life was not going to unfold as I might desire. The bottom line for me was to heal all the pain and the guilt, and I knew this couldn't happen if I wasn't willing to see the truth.

How my current anger toward men stemmed from the last life became a little clearer. I was a soldier. I had to have been present during killing and abuse. Who am I kidding? I could feel that I had participated. And the uniform felt like one more layer of guilt. My perspective of this war continued to change. How could I, who I believe to be a decent person, have been on the side of the Germans, the perpetrators, the abusers? It didn't make sense.

While I was dealing with the shock of this realization I noticed that not only were people in body celebrating around the wall, but thousands of disembodied spirits were hovering over and near, and they were also celebrating. It felt as if the fall of the wall had released them and they were finally free. The day the Berlin Wall came down, the hearts of many souls, living and dead, were filled with joy and freedom.

.19.

The next several months were filled with reading and meditating on Germany. I began to brush up on German and took a refresher course. I was exhilarated to be speaking German again. Just hearing the words of the language can make me feel very content.

Using the technique of the shamanic journey, I was traveling back into the German lifetime. But as intrigued as I was to look back at this lifetime, I was equally fearful. I knew there was something I needed to see but had the sense that I wouldn't be pleased with what it was.

Frequently my journeys took me into very traumatic scenes such as stepping into air raids in Berlin or battlefields. In one journey I'm standing in the middle of the aftermath of a battle. It must be the Russian front. The snowy landscape stretches for miles. It is so cold. Everywhere I look the snow is stained red.

It's deathly still. Smoke rises from the ruined machinery. Butchered, bloodied bodies are strewn about carelessly. No one moves; no one is alive. All the tanks have been abandoned, and it is as quiet as a graveyard. There is a cold wind that blows right through me. I can see my breath. I can almost see the wandering souls of the recent dead. I don't like being here and leave.

It was the silence in this journey that struck me the most. Eerily peaceful.

Continually in my journeys I would get to a certain point and be unable to see past it. It would get black. Fear was blocking me. Part of me was fearful that I would get lost in this time and never get back. Another part couldn't face the truth of that life. It was clear that I needed the guidance and protection of someone qualified to assist me with this dilemma.

.20.

I found a woman who practices shamanic counseling. Cathy would help me over the next several months to gain crucial information.

In our first session Cathy found that we would journey together and find a safe way for me to enter the darkness. She was told that the darkness not only had to do with what happened to me, but also with things that I did. Following this, I also reminded myself that I had the choice of whether or not to go further into a memory when it came up—that if it was too unpleasant or just not a good time, I could stop.

Another issue that continually came up in this work dealt with how my current relationships were often with people I knew in the last life. Relating to them now would often bring back memories for me. Sometimes memories would come up for these other people but not always. I have found over time that almost everyone I have been close with during the years I have worked on this were people that I knew from that life. I have heard that groups of people that have known each other in other lifetimes will often incarnate in the same geographic location. And so it would seem that this was happening with me.

In one journey, I traveled back to the war and found myself in my soldier's role on the eastern front. Along with other soldiers, I was pointing my rifle at a group of frightened women and children who were clinging to each other. Many of them wore bandannas in the way that eastern European women cover their heads. What I noticed the most was the fear in their eyes.

As I gazed at this group, one woman in particular stood out to me. Although she didn't appear as she does now, I knew instantly that this was Cathy. And then the order came and I began firing over and over, shooting into the crowd of innocents until none were standing. They were screaming for mercy as they fell. Shocked, I pulled myself out of this journey as fast as I could.

After the journey I relayed this information to Cathy. She told me that it didn't surprise her that she might have been a peasant who was murdered in that time. But she did not want to know more. She had a definite aversion to this time period. Two signs that someone is from a certain time are an extreme interest in the historical information of the time or an extreme aversion, not wanting to know anything of the time.

One of my girl friends in this current lifetime would use a bandanna to pull her hair back while she washed her face. I hated how she looked, and I would try to get her to take it off. But she would tease me with it. She knew it reminded me of those innocent civilians I had murdered, and she would toy with my guilt. But she also knew when to stop. In some ways it was good for me to laugh at times through this remembering, or I would totally lose myself. But laughing was only a temporary reprieve, and always the heaviness dominated.

.21.

Memories would also come up spontaneously. Watching World War II documentaries on television was a very powerful tool for triggering memory. Usually I would know I was experiencing a memory by the way my body felt. It knew when I was seeing something that I have known before. It was my gut feeling. I was very drawn to the "World at War" television series. Anything about the war in Europe had my full attention but the war in the Pacific did not intrigue me the same way.

Many times when I would least expect it, something in my everyday life would stimulate recall. I remember driving on the freeway one sunny summer day in the city and seeing billowing black smoke, apparently rising from a tire fire in the distance. And I matter-of-factly said to myself, "Oh, that's what it looks like when a city has been bombed!" This was about a week before I experienced the regression in which I saw dozens of columns of black smoke rising from the city of Berlin.

.22.

In October 1989, there was an earthquake in San Francisco. At that time my two brothers and my sister all lived in San Francisco. Like millions of other Americans, I was watching the World Series game that was being televised from Candlestick Park. I was shocked to see the picture start shaking, and then the signal was lost for several minutes.

When someone finally came on the air and announced that there had just been an earthquake in San Francisco I went into a panic. All I could think of was, "Oh no! Not again. I can't lose my family again!" I was incredibly worried that they were all dead. I called my mother on the phone, and I know I sounded hysterical. She was calm and told me to just be patient and that as soon as they heard anything they would call. Which she did within an hour; my family was safe and well. But during that hour I was glued to the TV, sitting on my bed, holding and rocking myself, praying for the life of my family, and feeling the intense pain in my gut of the loss of my German family. I couldn't bear to lose my American family too.

The intense emotion I experienced at the thought of losing anyone currently in my life mirrored the pain from the previous life. The strength of the emotion struck me. Over and over my current experiences seemed to meld with the last life, and it began to seem that the last life had never really ended. It was just continuing. I wondered, *when will this end? I can't bear this burden much longer.* This pain and, in a way, this responsibility were seemingly never-ending.

And then there was the time I was driving through the city and passed a building that was in the process of being torn down. It was a shambles. Chunks of concrete were in disarray, with the metal supports bent in defiance and rising out of the rubble, just as buildings look when they have been bombed. I glanced sideways out the car window, and my gut contracted in fear. Holding tightly onto the steering wheel, I had to tell myself, "It's okay; it's not what you think. The war is over. This is Salt Lake City. You are not in Berlin. It's over. That building has not been bombed; it's being dismantled intentionally. This is 1990. It's not happening again." And I took a couple of deep breaths and drove on. All the while part of me was not believing it was over.

.23.

The memories and reminders of this previous life not only affected my personal life, but had connections to my current career as a physical therapist, which began to be apparent through the clients with whom I was working. One client in particular gave me the opportunity to learn more about where my work was taking me.

It was while I was working at a nursing home that Helen Polonski came to me for physical therapy. She was in her seventies, and had had a stroke, which had affected her speech. She was unable to express herself. She was diagnosed with global aphasia, which meant she could neither speak nor understand what was said to her. But I was quite sure that she understood and could have responded but simply chose not to. She just had a look about her at times that told me that she was fully aware of what was happening but had made a conscious choice to act unconscious.

I'll never forget the first time I saw her. I walked into the therapy room. She was sitting on a mat on a low exercise table. As I walked toward her I heard myself out of the blue silently say, *"This woman has been in a concentration camp."*

She showed no emotion except when she first looked at me, and I could have sworn that she looked frightened. At that time I had very little information about my last life, and I thought the fear was simply due to her current medical situation. Now, though, I think differently. It was almost as if she recognized me.

She didn't follow verbal cues, and it was clearly going to be difficult to work with her. Her husband, a small man, was very concerned and almost fearful about her condition. Through him I discovered that they were both Polish and had been in the camps during the war. Although I don't ever remember discussing it, I was quite sure they were Jewish. He told me that they came to America right after the war.

It was odd working with Helen. I found myself having a greater need to help—wanting to connect with her—than I usually feel with clients. But to no avail. She was in her own world. After only a few weeks of therapy without much progress, we had to simply send her home. I never saw her again.

.24.

It was probably more than a year after this that I was cleaning out a file cabinet, and I came across my record of her treatments. I had quickly tossed out the other old charts I came across but this one wouldn't go into the wastebasket. For some reason I couldn't throw it away. So I just put it to the side.

I went about my day, but Helen was in my consciousness and wouldn't leave. By this time I was learning how to tell whether someone was in my space because they needed something from me or because I was putting them there. If I had the time, I simply would journey on it. But also I have found that if I give it a little time and they go away, then usually I was putting them there. If they don't, I need to pay attention and do something about it. By the end of this day Helen had not gone away, and I finally decided to journey on it.

I met with my spirit guides and told them what was happening, but as has happened before, they already knew and had simply been waiting for me to come. We traveled together to a place that was dark but in the earth plane.

Slowly I began to see a pair of eyes, and I knew immediately that this was Helen. And then there were several other pairs of eyes. That was all that I saw. Just eyes with darkness all around. And then Helen spoke to me and told me that she had died but was stuck in the earth plane. And the people around her now were members of her family that had died in the camps, who had been waiting for her since that time. But none of them could move on to the light yet because members of their family were still stuck in the camps. They needed someone to travel to the camp and bring them back to the rest of the family. And that someone was me.

My initial reaction was, "Oh no, not me! I'm not going to a concentration camp. You'll have to find someone else!" But my spirit guide calmly told me that yes, I was to do this, that there was nothing to fear, and that it was part of my destiny to do this work.

Well, I realized what needed to be done, and I was capable of doing it. I had already been trained in assisting stuck souls moving to the light. So with my power animals I put out the call for Helen Polonski's family and traveled to the concentration camp where they were. I don't know which one it was but it felt like Germany. I remember noting what it looked like physically because the thought entered my mind that I would probably be there some day in body.

I was really struck by how many souls were wandering aimlessly in this place. I saw hundreds, and many came towards me wanting my help but I knew that it was very important that I only bring back members of Helen's family. I had to tell the others to wait, that I or someone else would return to assist them.

So I continued to look for Helen's family and what appeared was a very young girl, perhaps four or five years old and a boy not much older. They were both very shy and very sad, and they were Helen's children. I told them who I was and what I was doing. I told them that it was time to go home. Their faces lit up; they were very excited. Holding them each by the hand we flew back to the place where the rest of the family was waiting. When they were reunited there was so much joy even I began to cry.

They quickly came together and formed a ball of light energy. Their individuality was lost. I had a crystal with me, and I told them to enter the crystal to the light. With the apex of this quartz crystal pointed to the heavens, they entered as a group. Out of the top an incredible beam of white light shot straight up, and in the light were what looked like little stars. I thought maybe those were the individual souls. And there was such a feeling of joy that it was almost overwhelming. This family had waited fifty years for this!

It was clear to me that this was a soul group and that they could not have moved on to the next plane of existence until they were all together. It was incredible. I almost thought I heard giggling from the beam that rapidly moved up to the heavens.

I was so honored that I had been allowed to have a part in this. And I realized my initial hesitation was silly. What an incredible healing this was to experience! And it gave me a clue about where this work was to take me. Maybe something good and joyous might come from all this pain and suffering.

.25.

I have had the assistance of many along this journey into the past, friends and healers—perhaps all friends in some way. It seemed that each person entered my life precisely when I needed them and they needed me.

In the spring of 1990 Lori entered my life. I had never known someone so sensitive and soft before. She really epitomized femininity to me. It was her gift, and sometimes her burden, to be incredibly empathetic. She honored the depth of feeling I had around all the memories, and she could feel what I felt. She helped me to feel validated and not crazy.

She also had a history of memory loss and then a slow recall of an abusive childhood in this life. She knew what it was like to begin recalling something that had happened years before and to see how much these lost memories were affecting her current life.

She wasn't afraid when I would go into a memory. She would hold me and often help me through the process. Thinking back now, I don't know of anyone else who could have done this for me at that point. My depth of feeling frightened some. Others wanted me to get over it and move on. "Quit being so serious. Life is supposed to be fun. It was fifty years ago, it's over," was their advice.

Lori also had to deal with people who did not want her to honor her past. Some of her family members also remembered, but others did not want her past validated. The pain of invalidation! Trying to explain to another without any cold, hard facts, any hard evidence, often has left me feeling drained. Only those who have felt something similar can understand. And one thing I had to learn, and am still learning, is with whom to share this information and whom not to.

Lori came into my life as more than just a friend. She was a mirror to me of the guilt I continued to carry. I loved her deeply but she was married. The truth was that we had come together only to help each other to the next place, and then we would be on different paths.

Her marriedness was evidence to me of how I still felt undeserving of a full relationship with another person. I was frustrated with this and actually tried to stop the relationship in the beginning but destiny was greater than my personal will. We had things we had come together for, and those were more important than my fear of having to go through another inevitable breakup.

She was also someone that I had known fifty years previously. We had known each other in Berlin as friends. Actually we both felt strongly that we were probably lovers. More than once while making love in this life we would both flash back to Berlin and remember having been lovers there—as a man and a woman! This was another example of how the boundary between lifetimes can be blurred. It was also an example to me of how one falls in love with a soul, not a sex!

.26.

During the time of this relationship with Lori I continued my past-life regression work through the technique of the shamanic journey. In one particular journey I traveled back to wartime Berlin. I found myself in the middle of an air raid. It was incredibly frightening as bombs were falling all around, and the sounds of the explosions were horrendous. It's no wonder I have been so frightened by lightning and thunder in this life. They are too much like the sounds of war.

Anyway, this raid was in the middle of the day, and people were scrambling in a panic trying to seek shelter from the openness of the street. There must have been very little warning. One woman in particular caught my attention. Even though I was looking at her back, I knew it was Lori as she appeared in the last life. She was wearing a brown skirt with a jacket and high heels. I felt myself wanting to call to her but my power animal pulled me back and reminded me I was only here to observe.

The bombs continued to fall and she was running down a flight of stairs that led to an outer basement door when a bomb fell right there and in a flash she was gone! Nothing left. Nothing! I watched in disbelief and shock. It happened so fast it was hard to comprehend the existence of a body one second and then nothing the next. When I shared this with Lori, she didn't doubt the validity of it, although she had no specific memory of how she had died in the last life.

Several months later I went to see a psychic. I had never been to an official psychic before and I was curious. The information that was revealed to me through this woman would be major pieces of my puzzle. Our session began with a disturbing question.

"Are you Jewish?"

"Why would you ask me that?"

"Because you look Jewish," she said rather matter-of-factly. "I've found over the years that often people will incarnate looking like those they persecuted in a previous life."

Well, I was very uncomfortable with this information. I shared with her the healing work I was doing which involved looking at the last life.

"It's no accident that you have come to see me," she said. "I have done readings on hundreds of people that were from the time of the 1930s and 1940s. In fact, I think most of the baby boomers are from that time. Think about it! Fifty million people died in that war. That's a lot of souls!"

Somehow I was feeling comforted by what she was saying.

She continued, "There were many victims of World War II."

Feeling embarrassed with that information, I had to say, "Well, I wasn't one of the victims. I was on the other side." I hated having to admit this.

She looked me straight in the eye and said, "Fifty million people died in that war. Every person who died was a victim— including all of the Nazis!" I sat back feeling stunned and speechless. *I was a victim?*

She went deeper into her space and began to describe me as I looked when I was a young German boy.

"I see a young boy wearing a uniform. It has an arm band with a swastika on it. You have on shorts and you're wearing a tie. It looks like the uniform of a Hitler Youth."

I felt the heaviness of this truth. First I had to accept that I was a German male but hopefully a civilian. And then that was shattered with the realization I was in the army. But to be more a part of the Hitler machine was very difficult to own.

And there was more.

"I'm sensing that there is some kind of a secret behind the uniform," she said as she went deeper into trance. "The uniform was an attempt to hide something about your family." She paused for a moment and then said, "I'm seeing your mother now. Oh, now I understand. Did you know that your mother was Jewish?"

"No!" I said.

"Do you realize what this means?" she asked.

"I'm not quite sure," I replied.

"In Judaism the line is carried by the mother. Whether or not your father was Jewish wouldn't have mattered. It means that you were Jewish!" she informed me.

I was Jewish! How I was able to get into the Hitler Youth I don't know. The idea of a Jewish boy in the Hitler Youth was at first unbelievable to me, but later I would find through reading and a very profound movie, "Europa Europa," that there were Jewish people hiding right under the noses of the Nazis. What better way to hide your Jewishness than by looking like as patriotic a German family as possible and having your son a member of the Hitler Youth? And so the feeling of having to hide who I am begins here.

A few days later Lori and I had a session together with the psychic. The reading began with the way that Lori came into this lifetime. She had come spiraling in rapidly. When her spirit came into form it was hurtling, similar to the way she had exited the last lifetime. We sat listening as the reading continued.

> *"It is somewhere in eastern Europe in a big city. All day you had been feeling 'off.' You had a sense that things weren't right. There is a great commotion in the streets. It is as if everyone has been caught off guard. I see you running down some stairs, and there is a great flash of light and you are gone. Hurtling, spiraling into space as you leave your body. It is as if you have been ejected."*

Lori and I looked at each other with amazement. She was the only other person I had told about the journey of her death, and here we sat listening to someone describe exactly what I had seen. It was an extraordinary revelation but it also felt as if I had somehow been violated. Someone was describing an event that I had experienced in a very internal and private space. But, in truth, the information was out there for anyone to tap given the right tool. The information was not mine. I had tapped into it just as the psychic had.

I realized that this information was a confirmation for me of the other information about myself that the psychic had revealed. If I was having doubts about having been in the Hitler Youth and being Jewish, they were crumbling. Every now and again the universe gifts me with a sign to trust what I am receiving.

Although the relationship with Lori was destined for only a short term, the timing of her entry into my life was no accident. She was a great support for me. She understood what it was like to experience a flashback. This kind of support goes beyond words. It is important to have someone honor your experience, to allow you to have it, and perhaps most of all, to be an anchor.

For me, one of the greatest fears of exploring the past has been of getting lost in it. I often felt that the deeper I went into a memory, the less chance there was of coming back. And there may be some truth to this, so a support system is vital. Also the technique I used the most for going back, the shamanic journey, gave me a specific way of entering the past, and even more importantly, the way to get back here.

.27.

Two years and six months after my first trip to Berlin, I returned in the middle of winter—January 1991. It seemed appropriate that I would return in the time of long nights of darkness.

When I returned in 1991 I knew more about myself in this past time and was returning consciously for healing. I carried the intention of finding my family's home. I wanted to do some kind of completion to honor this family's passing.

In the interim I had gained more knowledge but there were still gaps missing. I had realized and began accepting, although sadly, that I had been a German soldier who had fought on the eastern front. I had remembered being wounded in the abdomen in a battle there. The field hospital I had been taken to was attacked, and I escaped the bomb blast by seconds. Men who could not ambulate died in their beds, despite the large red cross on the roof of the hospital. Nothing was sacred in this war—on either side.

But I also remembered my hand in the killing of civilians, something that even today is difficult to own but truthfully felt.

And I saw people I loved die.

But there was a twist in this unfolding story—things were not black and white. How complicated and unbelievable things can become—imagine being Jewish and actually fighting for Hitler! My mother was Jewish. I was Jewish. It was the family secret. It was to be kept secret if the family was to survive. The plan to hide this was to have me join the Hitler Youth. I guess in a way it was like hiding out in the open. By the age of seventeen I was in the war. I was stunned by this information and almost found it unbelievable. A Jewish boy in the Hitler Youth! But I have read accounts of Jews hiding out among the Nazis, and the movie "Europa Europa" was like watching my life flash before me.

But this issue of hiding the truth of who I was, who my family was, in the face of death and then in the end losing all anyway has deeply ingrained in me the need to be true to who I am this time around. I really do feel now that I would rather die than hide the truth of who I am. And I do hold a truth that some might say would be better left in the closet, so to speak, but this I cannot and will not do. I am a lesbian, and in the face of those who would try to say I am an aberration, a sickness, a disease that must be eradicated, I will stand up for the natural and normal part of humankind that I am.

If it is possible to say that something positive came from the holocaust, it would be that in the face of the most systematic killing process ever created by human beings to destroy other human beings, the truth of the Jewish race was not destroyed. Truth cannot be killed. Human beings can be killed but the truth of who they are will not die. And so I would rather stand for truth and die because I know it will go on. The body I inhabit will cease to exist at some point, but the truth of who I am will continue.

The Jewish people continue and homosexuals always have been and will always be. I have this image every now and again that a few centuries from now people will look back at this time and wonder how it was that people could be so closed-minded and fear-driven in their attitude toward homosexuality. I was listening to a talk show recently, and a few people from Holland on the show were asked about their attitudes towards homosexuals. Their response was basically, "You Americans are still dealing with that?! It was long ago accepted by us as a normal part of being human." Holland, I think, is a few light years ahead of the rest of us, in many ways.

But to continue. I had been using shamanic journeying to make a map of where I had lived in eastern Berlin. I had some information but it was rather sketchy. I thought that by actually being there, perhaps the information would simply come back to me.

I had a street name, Voyersicherstrasse. This didn't make any sense to my German friend Paula or Ingrid, who would open her house to me in Berlin. Even now, I think that the street sign I saw in my journey was difficult to read because of the German script. I can't always read German words in ordinary reality in this script.

I had a name, Hans Grunewald. I saw Grunewald on the building of the apartment my family lived in. I have had thoughts of trying to find my official records. As a soldier of the German army, I must be on record somewhere in Germany. But this is not the most pressing thing and will simply come in its time.

I knew that I wanted to do some kind of shamanic work in Berlin. I wanted to find a shaman that I could work with there. I contacted the Foundation for Shamanic Studies and was given the names of some people to contact. Through these people I was told of two women in Berlin who did shamanic work. One spoke some English and the other none.

I wrote a letter in German to the woman who spoke some English. Her name was Ingrid. I asked her if she knew of a place I could stay, and I told her a little about myself and my need to do shamanic work.

By the time I had to leave on my trip I had not heard from her and planned to contact her from Cologne. The first part of my trip would be spent there visiting Paula.

I was both excited and very nervous about this trip. I wished I didn't have to do it alone but also knew this was the only way.

.28.

In January of 1991 the United States had troops in Saudi Arabia and was getting ready to retake Kuwait from Saddam Hussein. War was imminent. Leaving Salt Lake, I traveled to Dallas for the connecting flight to Frankfurt. There were many people in uniform waiting to board the same flight. Some were women. I have always felt perplexed by women in military uniform, which seems like a contradiction in terms. To me women represent the future of the planet. They are bringers of peace and nurturers. They are wholeness and love. To participate in patriarchal warmongering is regression, as I see it. But anyway, it was also the simple sight of military uniforms heading in the same direction I was that frightened me. There never will be a war to end all wars. Fifty years after the biggest war the planet has ever experienced, it still continues.

This occurrence brought the experience of war too close for comfort. Even as I walked down the gangway to board the plane it took a lot of strength to not turn tail and run. It was as if I were split. Part of me tried as hard as it could to run away, and the other part had to fight just as hard to keep me headed forward. It was only a matter of seconds but it was obviously a place of great choice for me. I could have turned around and left all of this behind and simply gone on with my life with a different emphasis. But I didn't turn around. I chose to enter the darkness. Sometimes I still have a hard time believing I found the courage to make that choice.

Once I made it on the plane, the flight itself was long but uneventful, and I arrived in Frankfurt in the morning. After going through customs I made my way down a few flights of stairs to the train station directly under the airport and boarded the train for Cologne. The train traveled northward along the Rhine. It was tranquil and beautiful here. There was no snow, which seemed odd to me in the middle of winter. Looking to the right, I could see the river, and to the left bluffs rose up to great heights. Little towns and houses were embedded on the hillside. Hints of castles lay in the distance.

And then I saw a line of old boxcars sitting vacant on idle railroad tracks. *Oh no, I can't look.... Make yourself look.* A shudder passed through me. *I've only been in Germany a few hours, and already the past comes haunting me. Remember, it's over. No one is in those boxcars. It's okay. It's over.* I breathe a sigh of relief but feel an omen of foreboding. Can't turn back now, though.

.29.

Paula met me at the station in Cologne. How wonderful to see a familiar face! However, by this time I was feeling weak and nauseous. I think it must just have been the long trip. My first twenty-four hours in Cologne were spent almost entirely sleeping. I was exhausted. It took so much emotionally and mentally to get myself there—and this was only the beginning. I wasn't sure I would make it through the next three weeks.

The time I spent in Cologne was difficult. It was difficult for Paula also, as I wasn't entirely happy to be there. And I think it was hard for her not to take this personally. We talked about this, and although she admitted she couldn't really understand the work I was doing she supported me, and that meant a lot.

I felt such heaviness in Cologne. I went for runs in a park where there were many older people walking and exercising their dogs. The weightiness I felt from them was immense. And their eyes were tired. I would want to say "hello" or "morgan" or whatever, but people would just look at me with no expression. It was very cold. Perhaps this is how all big cities are, but Cologne isn't exactly New York or Berlin.

Paula was working most of the time I was there, so I was left on my own. In reality I didn't want to sightsee. It didn't feel very pleasurable to me. To get to museums and the center of town one needed to take the bus or train, and this was very difficult for me. I have always had trouble with public transportation but in Germany it was worse. I have this fear that I will get trapped and not be able to get off where I need to.

When I was six years old and in kindergarten I got on the wrong bus one day to go home. I was paralyzed with fear. I just sat there as every stop looked unfamiliar. I stayed on the bus not saying a word. Finally the driver had to get me to tell him where I lived, and he took me home. The fear this experience instilled in me has never left me. It's a fear of being taken to a strange place where I know no one and that somehow I can't get back home.

So most of the time in Germany I would walk, even if it meant walking for miles. I would see the bus or train passing by me that I could be on, but I couldn't get myself to get on it. If I was with Paula, I would get on and feel a little better but not normal as one should be. She was very perplexed by this and would get impatient with me.

One Sunday Paula, her boyfriend, and I drove out of the Cologne city limits to take a walk in the woods near a small town called Aachen. I had never heard of Aachen before. It is a very old town from medieval times. The Dom or cathedral in its center was from the 1200s.

Our walk in the woods was somewhere outside of Aachen. There was a place for people to park their cars, and then everyone would go off on the trails into the woods. As we walked I felt more and more melancholy and had a feeling of going deep inside myself. It is always difficult for me to interact with people when this happens; I guess it's like trying to be in two worlds at once.

We walked around for quite a while. I created some distance between Paula and her boyfriend and me. They had a very intense relationship and seemed to be having another argument, and I didn't want to be involved. I began to have strange sensations in my body. My camera was strapped over my right shoulder, and I had to keep looking at it to make sure it was a camera because in my mind I kept seeing a rifle strapped over my shoulder. It was weird.

After a while a small airplane began flying overhead, doing stunts and circling around in a small area. Once again, I had to fight the instinct of my body. I wanted to dash for cover because it felt dangerous to be seen in the open. This was really weird. I was with other people, and I couldn't go diving into the bushes, although it was such a strong urge it took great willpower not to give in to it.

The trees and surroundings looked strange and familiar at the same time. I noticed how the leaves on the trees looked different from any I had ever seen before. And yet they didn't.

When we finally left I was rather relieved but confused. I couldn't explain this incident at all. I had expected weird things to happen in Berlin but not here. I wanted to leave Germany. The longer I was there, the harder it was to stay, and I hadn't even gotten to Berlin yet. I just wasn't sure I could handle what might come up for me.

Later I learned that Aachen and the surrounding woods was where the allies entered Germany towards the end of the war. There had been a battle in the woods. I saw a documentary, and it showed soldiers running through the woods and fighting, the same woods and hills I had walked with Paula and her boyfriend. And I realized instantly, that of course I had been there before!

I was feeling very overwhelmed with simply being in Germany, and I had to keep telling myself that just being there was enough. If nothing more happened it was okay. It was a struggle to maintain my energy level. I felt very drained. It was hard to think about doing anything beyond maintaining myself and breathing.

From my journal of January 16, 1991:

"Why am I in Germany at this time—when the world seems to be on the brink of another war? Is it simply coincidence? I don't feel that I am accomplishing much on a personal or world level.

"I'm trying to keep myself calm and to remind myself that to simply be here is enough. I have a light within but it is difficult to feel it. I feel so overwhelmed by the energy of this place. And

I don't even really know what the energy is. I just know that I feel depressed, low on energy.

"It is hard for me to get myself to do spiritual work. I did journey today. My lion showed me great fires in a distance. (Now I realize these were oil fires in Kuwait!!!!) I had the feeling that these fires were inevitable. The rest of the journey I spent in a circle with many animals of the forest. My lion was very gentle with me and affirmed that it was enough to simply be here."

The next day the war started. And in my journal I wrote: "The start of another war, and I am in the same place as I was when the last big war started! What a drag."

The feeling of the war was very close, as Germany is connected by land to Iraq and Saudi Arabia, albeit at a great distance. This made me realize how buffered the United States has been from war. There has always been an ocean separating it and allowing the reality of war to be unreal. Only the combatants could know the truth of the situations from the Ardennes to Vietnam. And no wonder their reintegration was difficult in a society that had no concept of what they had been through.

Another situation occurring in Germany that was unsettling was anti-American protesting in the cities because of the language barrier. I was already feeling like an outsider in Germany, and now outward protest was being directed against America. Banners were draped from buildings, and people in the streets carried signs that said "Kein Blüt Fur Öl" (No Blood for Oil). I was angry at these protestations, not so much because they were anti-American, but because they hadn't occurred when Saddam Hussein invaded Kuwait. Where were these people then?

I saw on the television how people were protesting en masse in Berlin. My hesitation about going there was now greater. It was not looking like a very warm and inviting situation to enter.

Before leaving for Berlin I did make contact with Ingrid's daughter Nadia. She spoke English and was very nice. And in fact she offered me a spare room in their apartment while I was in Berlin. Their kindness was very comforting.

.30.

After spending the first two weeks of my three-week trip in Cologne I finally made my way north. The train would take eight hours to get to Berlin. To be honest, I don't remember much from this ride. I was nervous and anxious.

When the train entered the land that was once East Germany, I could feel it. I don't know what it is exactly, but the energy of the east, of Communism, is palpably different from the modern west. And the people getting on the train were noticeably different. They appeared poorer to me in many ways. Energetically they didn't display the confidence of who they were as West Germans do. West Germans seem proud of who they are; but the East Germans carry shame. And perhaps they felt the heaviness even more as they boarded a train coming from the west. Once again the eyes were lowered and the smiles sparse. I remembered Paula saying how she felt the two Germanies were two different countries, and I had to admit that I could see what she meant on this train.

It's amazing what a wall can do to human beings. Losing contact with one another creates division and differences, creates two different worlds.

The trained slowed into Magdeburg, a small town with buildings showing their wear—blackened with time, worn, tired. Leaving Magdeburg, the train crossed a deep ravine, and I could see the remnants of the original bridge running parallel with our course. The vertical concrete placements, seemingly defiant, were all that was left, connecting the deep recesses of the ravine with only air. The horizontal aspect of the bridge had been missing for fifty years. Once again I was mesmerized by this reminder of the destructive past and couldn't turn my head. It was as if the bridge was trying to speak, to cry out, but no one was listening. No one but me even noticed it was there.

And then it was left behind once again.

And now we were approaching Berlin from the west. It was very woody and there were many gardens with little houses on them—shacks really. Then more and more buildings and the train slowed as we entered the city. Home. Even with all my nervousness of what was to come, I can't help but feel the joy of coming home. I hope I never lose that feeling when I go back to Berlin.

An older woman shared the compartment with me for most of the trip. She was quiet, almost shy, and kept to herself. I felt a warm feeling for her but I was nervous about attempting my German, and I held back. I think she knew I was an American and she spoke no English. As we approached the Zoo station in Berlin she struggled to get her luggage off the raised rack. Without thinking, I asked her, "Kann ich Ihnen helfen?" Can I help you? With a warm smile she acknowledged her appreciation. It was such a simple interaction and yet it was meaningful, as I still remember years later the positive energetic connection that occurred between us because of this small act.

From the Zoo I got a taxi to Ingrid's house. I couldn't believe this woman, whom I had never met, would open her house to me. She welcomed me with an open heart, and fortunately, with better English than my German. Her daughter Nadia, a university student studying American studies, was full of energy and life. They made me feel at home.

For the first few days back in Berlin I combed the streets, searching for clues to my former home. I revisited many of the sights that had stimulated a past life recollection during my first visit in Berlin two years earlier. But nothing was coming through.

Of course I felt comfortable and familiar but there was nothing to indicate new revelations.

On the eastern side I was amazed at the commercialization that had already occurred. Expensive clothing stores stood along the Unter den Linden, obviously there only for the Western shoppers. Former Communists could never dream of affording these things.

I walked and walked until I was exhausted. I looked so hard for any kind of a clue that eventually I made myself sick. During the night of the second day I threw up several times. Feeling sick and weak the following morning, I received the message that I had been trying to take in too much, and my body literally had to release by vomiting.

I spent the morning writing and remembered that I had been told to allow my intuition to guide me as I wandered Berlin and realized that my effort up until then had been very mental. I had made a plan and decided I was going to make it work no matter what, even if I got sick. Well, it didn't work.

Now I realized I needed to allow spirit to guide me, and I had to calm and quiet my mind. Obviously this was another in the many lessons I have had of needing to let go of control!

.31.

The next day I took the only bus that traveled at that time between East and West Berlin. I took it as far into the eastern portion of the city as it went, which really wasn't very far, perhaps three miles at the most. I entered an area surrounded by dreary, characterless, Communistic apartment buildings. I stepped off the bus and saw a brick wall surrounding an area of trees. I felt drawn to this spot. Crossing the street, I noted the residents of the area awaiting public transport had no expressions except boredom. Their clothes looked at least ten years behind the times; many wore wide-legged pants!

As I walked along the outside of the wall I couldn't see what was inside until I rounded the corner and realized it was a cemetery. Instantly I understood why I would be drawn here. Perhaps my family had been buried here. I felt very strongly the need for completion around the murder of my family. I wanted to honor that they existed and that they died.

This cemetery was very old, with graves dating from the 1700s to the 1960s. Many of these people had died in 1945 just before the end of the war. I felt saddest for these who had almost survived the insanity. So close. Perhaps I was also feeling for my own family who had died in the final months of the war.

The feeling of almost making it but not surviving was hard to shake. And truthfully it still is. To realize that one moment has changed things forever. I can't help but think if that moment of murder could have been delayed just a little, it might have never happened.

I have this feeling of wishing I could change the past—of seeing scenes of people entering the showers in the camps and wishing that through my own will, I could turn the gas off forever and all these people would still be alive. They would go on with their lives and reunite with their families and friends. I just know it didn't have to be the way that it was, but I can't change it. I must accept that it did happen and is unchangeable. I mourn this loss to humankind. And every time I think I can't possibly have another tear to shed, there is more. There is more. There are always more tears.

And so I began exploring this densely populated cemetery. Row upon row of headstones stood here with lots of trees and bushes intermixed. I searched and searched for a grave marker with Grunewald engraved upon it. But nothing. I was so sure that my family was buried here.

As I walked, I moved into a depth of emotion that, until that time, I had not allowed to surface—the sadness of mourning this huge loss to my being. But this soon turned to anger. Anger at war. Anger at Hitler for leading Germany into this suicide. Anger at Germans for going along. Anger at Jewish people for falling for the ploy of relocation, for being so passive and not fighting back. And in the final months Hitler could have surrendered and saved thousands of lives, but no! According to this maniac, if Germany couldn't win the war then Germany did not deserve to exist. And Goddamn it! My family was only trying to survive. And even worse, I was fighting for this machine that was systematically killing the essence of who I was.

Isn't that a laugh! I was a Jew! And I was in the German army. And so finally the anger turned inward. My loss and my pain were encapsulated in a guilt that felt as if it could never be released. But I had done what I did in order to save my family and myself. The choices were few. And my father made the choice for me to join the Hitler Youth. How could he have known that in the end the roots of this movement would destroy us all?

The more I searched for their graves in vain, the more intense my emotions became. I finally stumbled upon the grave of a young German soldier. He had died in his early 20s, and written on the marker was, "Er gibt seinem leben für Deutschland" (He gave his life for Germany). Well, it was here that I really lost it. I was so angry. What absurdity that people felt he gave his life for this country! What a bunch of shit! I could only feel how robbed he was at losing his life so early.

I realized that it was here that I needed to perform a ritual. I couldn't find my family but I could bring the light to this young man. And so, after three hours of wandering this cemetery with tears in my eyes and an array of emotions emerging, I had found what I was looking for. I decided to return the next day with my candle and say a prayer for this man.

I left feeling uplifted. It wasn't what my mind thought I had come to Berlin for, but I could tell by the way my body felt that this was what I needed to do. It felt right and I felt energized and hopeful about completing something.

But things often don't work out the way you envision, and just when I thought I had reached the door, it slammed shut. I returned the next day, and try as I might, I could not find the grave again. I looked and looked. It was as if it had disappeared or was never there. Once again I searched row after row of headstones, disbelieving that I couldn't find what I thought was the reason I had been guided to this place. Again, anger came up, but before too long it was more a feeling of having been defeated. I was despondent.

I sat down on a bench and let the tears come. What kind of trick was this, that I would be led to this place and now it is not there? Now what?! And in my frustration I looked up and noticed the group of gravestones directly in front of me. There was another young man who had died in 1944, and all around him were the markers of people, civilians mostly, who had died in the last few months before the end. And the one that struck me the most was an entire family—seven names listed on the marker—ranging in age from three years to fifty years. Five of them had died on May 1, 1945, apparently in one of the last battles. The war had ended on May 8, 1945.

What insanity! My heart reached out to them. I was so sorry they didn't make it. It was here that I left my candle. I closed my eyes for a moment of silent prayer, then slowly rose and left the cemetery for the last time.

With each step my heart became filled with a joy I hadn't known before. I felt lighter. I was happy. I really didn't know what I had just done but my body was exhilarated. I must have done something! And I knew that I could return home with my mission accomplished.

That night I journeyed to the candle and was met by a group of small forest animals. The squirrels and rabbits were so happy to see me; they greeted me warmly and thanked me. I felt a little taken aback, not sure if I deserved this wonderful reception. And for the first time I could see the many spirits that were wandering the cemetery. It was not at all fearful; they were just there.

The animals told me they had been waiting a long time for someone to bring the light to this place and promised me that they would keep the candle lit. I was touched deeply by their care and concern. I asked about the first grave I had been looking for, and they told me that the young man there had already moved on to the light and didn't need my help. But the souls at the place I did leave the candle had been waiting, and now they have also moved on. Once again my tears flowed but this time with joy!

The cemetery's little protector animals were so warm and caring. Their presence helped me to understand how we in body must work in tandem with the spirit world. Alone, neither can complete the work, but together miracles are possible!

.32.

I packed my bags to return to Cologne the next day, still feeling exhilarated and just plain happy. It was such a good feeling to overcome something that I thought was not possible, especially when the path was not clear and all I could do was put one foot in front of the other and trust that I was going in the right direction. That was how this trip to Berlin was. I didn't know where I was going to go in Berlin; I just knew that I had to be in Berlin.

Even after I left the cemetery, I wasn't sure what it was that I had done. I felt as if I had stumbled my way through. I had this light but I didn't really know what to do with it. And by listening, I was guided. It was not necessary to have a mental understanding of healing. I knew by the way my body felt that it was accomplished. Lightness and joy cannot be artificially created.

I returned to the Zoo station, found the train heading for Frankfurt, and boarded. I knew the Frankfurt train stopped in Cologne. An older man who shared my compartment was leaning out the window saying his good-byes to an older woman standing on the platform. There was a very warm feeling between them and sadness at having to say farewell. As he turned around to sit down he smiled warmly towards me, and we exchanged greetings in German. He seemed very nice, and I didn't mind sharing my space with him. Normally I would have hoped to have the entire compartment to myself.

The journey began and we each tended to our own activities: I to my book and he to his radio with earplugs. A few hours passed and a steward came by offering coffee, and we each took a cup. And this obviously kind, older man made a light-hearted comment about how my coffee cup had a stripe around the rim and his didn't, which started us talking. He spoke some English, and with my minimal German, we began a conversation that was one of my greatest gifts.

"Have you been in Berlin for a vacation?" he asked pleasantly.

Not feeling prepared to be completely truthful, I simply replied, "I've been visiting friends."

After a slight pause I continued, "I like Berlin very much. I'm a little sad because I'm leaving, but I'm looking forward to coming back. Do you live in Berlin?" I asked.

A light appeared in his eyes and joyfully he said, "I was born in Berlin!"

Reminiscing, his eyes drifted from mine with a distant gaze. "Berlin was such a beautiful city before the war," he said with a smile. "On Saturdays I used to take long walks exploring the city. I loved going to museums. You know, Berlin had so many museums that one could take weeks visiting them and still not see all of them!"

The memory of the vitality of prewar Berlin was evident through his words and eyes. I could see how proud he was of old Berlin.

"I wish you could have seen it then," he said longingly.

If only he had known that as he spoke the memory was living again in my mind's eye! I could see people bustling about on the streets. I smelled the bunches of flowers for sale on the sidewalks. I looked up and saw the blue sky and felt the infamous Berliner Luft. I remembered Berlin when it was still innocent. I was there as he spoke.

I also remember wondering to myself how he knew that I was interested in old Berlin. Most Germans I had encountered did not want to talk about the past, or at the very least, did not share it freely. And yet he seemed to know, was almost concerned that I get this information.

"In 1943 my house was bombed in an air raid. It was completely destroyed," he said.

"Was anybody hurt?" I asked.

"No. No one was hurt, *Gott sei dank*," he said. "But now we were homeless and there was no place to live in Berlin. So many buildings were destroyed in the bombing. Many people were without a home. So my family left Berlin and went to Hamburg. They remained there until the end of the war."

He mentioned only briefly that he had been in the fighting, but this was something about which he did not want to go into detail, and I knew better than to ask about it further.

He had not returned to Berlin until now.

"I couldn't bear to see the city divided," he said. "And I especially could not bear to see the wall. It was much too painful for me." Tears began to well in his eyes.

He went on, "My home was in the eastern sector of the city. Now that the city is reunited, I came back to find the place where I had lived. I wanted to see it one more time."

I couldn't believe what I was hearing! When I questioned him further I found he had been back in Berlin for a week, the very same week I had been in Berlin searching for my house! The parallels were just too much.

Then he said, "You know, it's funny, I looked all over the area where I remembered living, and I couldn't find where my house had been!"

I sat there listening to this story totally amazed. He was still in the same body and had not been able to find where he had lived. How could I, who am in a new body, possibly have thought that I could find my house? And I realized in that moment that it was never intended that I should find my house. I felt relieved now because I had been disappointed about not accomplishing this goal.

The woman at the train station was his sister who had remained in Berlin. The love between them was obvious. He had seen her since the war because she would visit him where he now lived in southern Germany.

The thing that struck me most about this man was that there was no bitterness in his heart, only joy. He was not the typical

German I had encountered. He was very interested in talking and willingly sharing with me.

We continued to talk about other things for the rest of the trip, and the next five hours felt like one.

As we approached the end of the journey he asked, "So where are you going?"

"I'm going to Cologne. I have a friend there," I replied casually.

He looked concerned and said, "But this train doesn't stop in Cologne."

"Oops! I got on the wrong train!" I exclaimed.

Or so it would seem. It's very clear to me now that I had gotten on the right train. He helped explain to the conductor my dilemma, and for only a few Deutschmarks more, I was able to transfer to another train in Frankfurt that would take me the short journey to Cologne.

I'll never forget our farewell. He helped me with my bags and I got off the train. He came over to the window in the walkway of the train and pulled it down. I was standing on the platform. He leaned out the window and waved good-bye with a big smile. Even now, every time I think of that scene I start to cry. He touched me so deeply. And for some unknown reason we never shared our names with each other! He will always be a mysterious gift to me.

The next day I flew out of Frankfurt. I felt so light and wonderful, such a contrast to what I had felt at the airport in Dallas when I had the chance to turn around. Thank God I didn't.

.33.

A few days after I was back home in the United States, I went for a channeling.

"The greatest importance in your trip was the physical experience of remembering that you are multidimensional. The greatest importance of your memory of the forest, of the cemetery, of the air, of the texture of society, of the texture of the German people was the reinforcement of your knowing that you are more, on an experiential level rather than an intellectual level.

"The reason that this entire experience of your German past has been so predominant in your energy for these years of time and transition is so you could not release, you could not let go and intellectualize and say this was your imagination.

"The significance of the candle was the significance of your bringing the light into the situation. The significance of your interactions, of your train rides, of your walks, of your remembrances was the significance of this memory resonating reality to you that there is more than what we think. You have experienced this brilliantly on an intellectual level. It is the nature of your beingness to need to feel it in your body to know that it is so.

"How do you know that you love Lori? It's not simply a mental concept. It is a feeling deep within you, within your physical, mental, emotional, and spiritual self. This qualifies, determines to you that yes, I do love this person. I can feel it.

"How has this German saga of experience been so critical in your evolution and growth? Because you could make absolutely no sense of it but you could feel it. You could not intellectualize it. You could feel it. You could experience it."

"I still feel it now," I said.

"You will always feel it, as it is your constant reminder to trust that yes, I was with you. I am always with you. Not simply in Germany. I am always with you on some level. If you ask me to be with you, a cord of who I am, a string of who I am connects with who you are.

"However, you could feel it in Germany. You could experience it in Germany because you allowed yourself to experience being in an altered state of mind and walking in a physical reality, pretending you were normal, pretending everything was just normal. Kind of odd wanting to go to a cemetery to sightsee, nonetheless a historical, nostalgic type of thought.

"Yet the fact that you were alone and could feel and experience others around you gives you the information that you need. One of the keys to this experience in relationship with the course of shamanic study is the ability to release these individuals from the pain, the disorientation of sudden death."

"Is that what I did in the cemetery?" I asked.

"This is so. Is this not your experience?"

"Yes, but it's hard to believe that I can do such a thing!" I exclaimed.

"Simply, as you are speaking to me, we are utilizing the vehicle of Rayla [the channeler]. Yet, when you spoke to me in Germany I was simply a spiritual beingness, not coming through a physical voice. You knew that I was there. You knew that I was supporting you, connecting with you.

"In the same way you became the vehicle to voice, to say 'I know you are there. I can't see you but I came to give you a message. I don't know how to say it but it looks like this candle. And this candle simply is a representation of light. Look for this light and you will be home.' This is what you did.

"You were sent acknowledgement in many ways. However, you are so literal, as many are and rightfully so. You have been programmed to believe that there is not more than what you see in the basic senses, experiences. So a man was sent to you on a

train. *You had a normal conversation that was totally abnormal in another way. Yet on some level you were so connected with the other side of it, the nonreality of it rather than the reality of it, that you could see that this was an acknowledgement of what you had done, and you were an acknowledgement to him. You are not linear. There is not a beginning and an end. It is a continuum of thought, a continuum of experience.*"

As these words were spoken to me, the impact of their truth and the affirmation of the spiritual healing that occurred in me and around me brought a feeling of humility. I couldn't help but think that the man on the train was an angel. I've heard of that sort of thing, where an angel will appear at a particular moment to give a message, and then it is gone.

But also the thought that I had actually helped souls to move on was incredible. Maybe healing was possible out of all the pain and sadness I had experienced. Maybe something positive was going to come from all of this. Maybe the scars of the war could be healed—for the living and the dead. And maybe even for me.

.34.

From September of 1941 Jews were required by law to wear the yellow Jewish star on their clothing. As Jewish people in Berlin began to be rounded up for deportation, thousands went into hiding. They no longer wore the Jewish star and they became illegal. Many were hidden by ordinary German citizens who risked their lives in this undertaking. The Jews who went underground in this way were given the nickname "U-boat." Most of the U-boats were found or betrayed by war's end.

In order to decrease the chances of being found, U-boats would move from location to location, often spending only a night in one place and then moving on. The time spent in transit on the street was dangerous as they were visible.

The Nazis were not always able to detect a Jewish person simply by looking at them. But Jewish people were often able to spot each other. The Nazis used this to their advantage and employed Jewish people to hunt other Jews. They were called Greifers, or catchers. This made the situation of two Jews meeting in the street precarious, as one couldn't always know whether to greet the other. There would be eye contact and then a quick turning away, with the hope that they hadn't been detected. The fear of betrayal was ever-present.

I have witnessed a similar phenomenon as a closeted homosexual in this life. Many straight people cannot always detect a gay person, but gay people always seem to find each other. Before I was out of the closet, my reaction to being detected was a very uncomfortable feeling. I did not want to be seen as gay. I did not want to be exposed. Being in the closet as a homosexual in this life was like being a U-boat in wartime Berlin.

Hiding my identity stirs strong memories of the last life. Not speaking up for myself has not been healthy. I have felt fear and shame because of my sexuality. In conversations with physical therapy clients, for example, there have been times when the subject of homosexuality came up, and the clients very honestly expressed disgust and expected me to agree with them. Obviously they had no idea I was gay. To hear someone denounce a part of who I am affected me in a deep way. I would say nothing, especially early in my career. I was not prepared to come out at that time. Even though I showed no reaction outwardly, somewhere inside I was very angry and hurt.

The need to hide an aspect of myself has carried over from one life to the next. The way to heal myself would be to come out of the closet.

For most gay people the ease with which they can come out to the world is determined by the degree of acceptance from their families. This was true for me. In the last few years almost everyone in my immediate family, with the exception of my father, had come to know about my homosexuality, and I was very much accepted. My ability to be completely out was hindered by the fact that my family had a concern about my father not taking the news very well.

My father is a kind and loving man but he has had a history of being a bit of a bigot when it came to homosexuals. When I was around fourteen years old he and I were watching the evening news, and there was a story about homosexuals. I don't remember the topic; I just remember my dad sitting back in his chair and saying, "Damn faggots!" I never forgot that. As I came to realize my homosexuality, I knew I could never tell him.

.35.

My inability to release the burden of hiding myself created resentment, which only added to the resentment I already had towards my parents. All my life I have resented their telling me what to do and how I should do it. From their perspective they are not trying to control me; they are just trying to help, and there have been many times I have appreciated their assistance. It's a matter of striking the balance between being helpful and being controlling.

One day my lifetime of resentment poured out of me all at once, triggered by a seemingly innocent event.

My parents were visiting for a few weeks one August. The three of us own my house together, and they visit a few times a year. It started when my mother began to rearrange my kitchen. She couldn't understand how I could function in a kitchen where each thing was not in its proper place.

"Now you should have all your canned goods on one shelf and all the rice and pasta on another. Oh, and where do you keep your sugar and flour?" she asked cheerfully.

"What flour? I don't have any flour," I said, just slightly annoyed.

"How can you not have flour?" she asked quizzically.

"Beats me, but so far I'm surviving," I replied rather sarcastically. "But I do know where the sugar is, down below on the shelf with the cat food."

"What?!" my mother exclaimed.

"It's no big deal," I said. "So far I'm not meowing after I drink my coffee, and the cat isn't any more hyper than usual. So there hasn't been any cross-contamination."

"Would you mind if I rearranged your shelves?" my mother asked.

Hesitating, I felt something beginning to boil within me. "Yes, actually, I do mind. I like things just the way they are," I replied, gritting my teeth.

"Your mother is just trying to help," my father chimed in. He was sitting on the couch in the living room adjacent to the kitchen.

Earlier that day my father had been instructing me in the proper changing of the air filters for the heating system and various other household maintenance chores, and it was then that the sensation in my gut began to heat up. By the time my mother wanted to take over my kitchen, my emotions needed little prodding to reach the boiling point.

"You have to have things in a certain order and place, and there are tasks that simply must be done to maintain a household. As long as we own part of this place, that is how it has to be!" my father commanded.

"But I am the one who lives here. You only visit once or twice a year!" I exclaimed. "You can't tell me where to put things! You can't tell me how to live!" My anger was a volcano on the verge of erupting. The resentment of a lifetime was the magma determined to release itself.

"If you aren't willing to do things the way they should be done then maybe we should just sell this place, and you can live as you like somewhere else!" my dad declared.

"Fine! Maybe that is just what we should do," I responded. I was very angry at this point.

By this time my mother and I were both in tears. But I felt as I have all my life: it was two against one. There was no chance of winning this battle. I felt as though I was completely losing control, and the tears really flowed. I sat down, defeated.

The true source of my frustration had been in the depths of my consciousness, and up to this point had been unclear, but now it was coming into focus. The resentments of my life had become encapsulated in one issue. Realizing what it was, I looked at my mother and said, "This isn't what this is about. You know what I have to tell Dad."

She looked at me sadly yet seemed to understand, just as I had, what this was really about. Resigned, she said, "Tell him."

My dad looked a little confused. "Tell me. Tell me what? What are you two talking about?!"

I took a deep breath. "Dad, I don't know how to tell you this except to just say it." I paused. Whatever would happen now was out of my hands. "Dad, I'm a lesbian and I have been since I was born."

My father's expression changed from inquisitive to shocked. He looked at me rather blankly and then sat down, saying nothing.

I turned toward my mother and said, "I'm sorry, Mom."

She looked back at me with kindness and love and said, "It's okay, honey. You finally had to tell him."

When I woke up that day I hadn't decided, oh, today is the day I will tell my dad I am gay! In fact, until the few minutes before I spoke the words, I didn't know myself what was going to come out of my mouth.

He sat back on the couch for several minutes before speaking. My Mom and I also sat silently, not knowing what he would say.

Finally he turned towards me and said, "In a matter of five minutes my whole world has turned 180 degrees. Up until now I thought homosexuality was something that a person chose and that it was sick. But you are a decent, caring human being and I can see in your heart that this was not a choice, that it simply is who you are."

He walked over to me and put his arms around me and said, "I love you, Maryanne. I love you with all my heart!" My mother joined us and we shared a wonderful group hug. All of us were crying.

In a matter of a few moments the already loving relationship between my father and me grew tenfold. A huge weight was lifted from my family. For the rest of the evening the three of us joked and talked about everything. I told my Dad about my book and the past-life experience. And about the times I had brought someone special to dinner.

"So Lori was your girl friend?!" he asked.

"Yes," I said.

Recalling that dinner, he said fondly, "I really liked her."

When it was time for bed we hugged each other once again and reflected on the evening.

My Dad said, "I feel as if I'm the one who has been in the closet for thirty years! Everyone knew about you but me. I'm glad I'm out!"

"That was one of the worst fights we've ever had," my mother said. "But I guess you could say it was worth it to get your father out of the closet and this family closer," she added, giving my father a wink and a smile. Turning towards me she said, "And, honey, I promise I won't ask to rearrange your kitchen again."

We all laughed. I could feel how much my parents loved and supported me. I will never again hide who I am.

I realize how empowering and important the support of one's family is. When you know they love you for who you are, the way the rest of the world reacts becomes a much smaller matter. I can't say that it doesn't matter at all. But each time I tell someone I am gay it gets easier. I have the sense that being truthful about who I am is helping me to heal the guilt of the last life.

.36.

In the middle of writing my story I find that I need to pause and reflect on what I am writing and why. I have read several personal accounts by all kinds of people from the war: Germans, Poles, Russians, French, Dutch, and of course Jews of many nationalities. Each has gripped me in its telling. And the question has to be asked: why are these stories important? Because the truth must be told and remembering made possible—all of the remembering.

There is talk these days that the holocaust was a hoax, that it was something made up by Jewish people to discredit Gentile-dominated culture and Nazism. This is very dangerous. If we do not remember the past we are doomed to repeat it.

The end of World War II did not end fascism. The mentality of Nazism has not faded. It has only changed form. Neo-Nazis can be found even in the northwest United States wanting to create their own country, and in the process they are threatening anyone who is different from them with bodily harm, all the while denying this fact. Black men have been lynched in the northwest. A Jewish talk radio host was assassinated in Denver, Colorado. And there was a bombing in Oklahoma City. Blacks, Jews, homosexuals, beware. You are not wanted, and if you do not leave we will remove you. That is the fascist story.

My writing about my remembering is not sensationalism. I did not do this because it was fun. Although it has been fascinating, it has been incredibly painful to work through the past. But I have never felt much choice in all this. It is clear to me that I cannot move forward in my life until I have dealt with this past.

Whether this story is read by one or one hundred people, I had to tell it. It is not important to me that anyone believes what I tell. My job is not to teach about the possibility of reincarnation and the implications of past lives. For my life it is simply truth.

Telling my story is not about dwelling in the past. This time in the 1940s has much to do with where the planet is and where it is going. It has much to say about how little or how much people have learned in fifty years. The longer I live, the more saddened I am to see it is more the former than the latter. I sacrificed my soul to live through a horrendous time, hiding the truth of who I was by denying and participating in the killing. And I will not be silent this time as I witness the injustice and the hatred. And I will not hide from it.

But this I must also say. No one who did not live through that time and place can understand what it meant to find a way to survive. Do not be quick to judge. Do not be quick to judge anyone who acts immorally under duress. One can only truly understand the immense desire of the human soul's will to live when faced with its termination. The need to survive can override all previous thoughts of morality and dignity. I do not say this to justify immoral acts. But I have found that I could only forgive myself when I felt compassion and understanding for my behavior. That with what I had to work with in that time, my skills as a human being, and the incredible pressures of the circumstances, those were the choices I made. Would I make them now? I hope not. I have much more self-knowledge now.

I do not ask for anyone's forgiveness. I know it is my own that is the most important. I am not ashamed of what I have revealed to myself about my past. Instead the memory carries great sorrow and loss. Sorrow for the people I loved who lost their lives before their time. Sorrow for the millions slaughtered. Guilt that I stood by and did nothing to save them and, in fact, participated in the killing. I wish that this had been different. I wish that I could explain away why. But I am at a loss. I bear this burden.

It may be difficult for some to understand how I could feel so much emotion around something that happened in another time, another place, and through another body. But my soul remembers as if it were yesterday. And I write this for those who also have a sense of that remembering. Healing is possible. And amazingly, it is not just about healing an aspect of the past, for the traumas of that terrible time were carried into the next life. And so, many of the problems and dysfunctions of my current life have been healed with the healing of this most recent past life.

With a frustrated heart I see that the hatred continues. I will not stand idly by this time. I am not afraid to be seen as Jewish or homosexual this time around. I am not afraid to be seen as who I really am.

But again I ask, why do I write this? In my own time it is so unbelievable. And from a past life even more unbelievable. And honestly there have been many times when I have not believed myself. My mind has struggled, tried to tell me that my story could not possibly be true. But the gut feeling in my body has absolutely no doubts of its truth.

My writing involves much more than simply telling the story. It has challenged my core being to question who I really am. I keep coming up with the answer that I am more than my mind could ever comprehend. And the people who surround me are more than my eyes can see. My awareness of the information my body has about people and places in my life has become a key for me. I am learning to listen.

I appreciate my mind. It has gotten me through my schooling. But it is only one part of me, and it is the place that carries fear and doubt. I must constantly reassure it that everything will be okay. It's getting calmer but still needs (and probably always will) comfort and support from me. In the end it is the quiet truth of my heart that I must honor first.

.37.

In the months following my return from Berlin new energy began to enter my life. Until this trip I had been using the technique of shamanic journeying for my own healing, but through a series of dreams and guidance I was told that it was now time to begin using this form of healing for others. This aspect of the work began in the cemetery in eastern Berlin. I was being drawn to working with the dead and those approaching death. This fascinated me but I was hesitant.

So much of this past-life work had been preparing me for working with death and its surrounding issues. Reliving my own death in the snow showed me the incredible peace and calm that can follow. The gift of having experienced the joyful reunion of Helen's family, and the reunions of one soul after another that I had known previously, cemented in me the knowing that death is not the end. It is the process of moving toward what is next. This does not negate the difficulty and sadness in having to say good-bye to someone. But I began to see how there is no finality in farewell, only a temporary separation. This has removed for me the fear of death as the end. At this point I really have no idea if there ever is an end to soul existence.

I also have the sense that there is no judgment following death—no hellfire and brimstone, just acceptance and peace. And as I began to journey more to the other side, my comfort level increased. So now as I sit with someone approaching death I can look them in the eye, and we connect soul to soul. In that moment I convey to them that they will be met and they will continue. The fear and the judgment is really only on this side.

.38.

One of my first teachers in this process was a man called Lorenzo. He was the first of many individuals that I would have the honor of working with as they moved into their deaths. Lorenzo had been a vibrant, life-loving man but by the time I met him, infections resulting from the AIDS virus were beginning to take their toll. He had generalized muscle weakness, and although he was still able to walk, his balance was tenuous at times. His spirit, however, remained strong. He welcomed me into his home, and we began our time together with exercise to attempt to regain what had been lost.

Lorenzo was one of the most gentle men I have known. Over time, a bond developed between us. I think we both looked forward to our sessions. Even if what we talked about did not have much substance I would always leave feeling energized and uplifted for the rest of the day.

After the first month or so it became clear that exercise was not going to ward off the disease process. He could no longer manage the stairway between the main floor and the finished basement where we usually worked. Eventually he became confined to bed. Although he never complained, it was clear that he was having discomfort in his body. It seemed silly to continue doing exercise, and I began to practice hands-on techniques to try to increase his comfort level. He was very open to trying new things.

The peacefulness that would envelop him following a session surprised me at first. I didn't feel I was doing that much. But then I realized that, of course, it wasn't me at all! So I focused on being a vehicle for healing energy to move through me to Lorenzo. More than once following our time together, when he was too weak to speak, he would look deeply into my eyes and a tear or two would flow from his. This gratitude, this feeling of connection beyond words, will never be forgotten by me.

When he was stronger Lorenzo would often talk about his mother, who had died a few years previously. When he became bed-ridden I sensed a beautiful woman with long flowing dark hair lingering in an upper corner of his bedroom. I was sure it was his mother, and this was later confirmed by his sister's description of her.

As death was nearing I sensed more and more beings in the room. They were just there holding a quiet vigil, very patient and very loving. Their presence was reassuring, and I knew that Lorenzo was in communication with them.

The last few days before his death Lorenzo slipped into a coma, but he would be restless at times. The hands-on sessions would calm him down for a few hours, and his family very much wanted me to continue them. Lorenzo was no longer available for communication except through touch. I allowed myself to go into an altered state and communicate with him through journeying.

He wasn't resistant to death. He was ready. Although he put on the face of a fighter for the last few months, it was mostly for his family. He had been preparing for the inevitable for some time now. So in another dimension we talked about the process of leaving the body and what would follow—of looking for the light and going for it. Lorenzo had so much spiritual support there really wasn't much for me to say. I just assured him that it was okay to go, that his time here was done. I talked a lot with his partner and sister and reassured them about the process. His sister was very sorry to see him leave but was able to let go. His partner was another story.

Bill was very loving and devoted to Lorenzo and could not let him go. He fought his death until the end and was in for a long mourning process. We spent many evenings together following

Lorenzo's death talking about what it all meant. At that time Bill did not have a sense of the afterlife, and his feeling of having lost Lorenzo forever could not be consoled. I had to eventually move on and leave Bill to his process. I hope his burden has been lightened with time.

Lorenzo died on my birthday. Bill called me that Saturday morning and asked if I would come, as it seemed that Lorenzo's time was close. I said "of course" and was there by noon. Lorenzo was sleeping peacefully and was demonstrating the changes in breathing that sometimes occur before someone dies. Mainly he would stop breathing for several seconds and then follow this with a period of rapid breathing. This would continue throughout the day.

I sat with Lorenzo doing the hands-on and working energetically with him. As I worked around his abdominal area I noted quite a bit of energetic activity. It was as if there was a great pulsing beneath my hands. As I moved up his body it diminished. But as the day went on I noticed that the energy began to move up towards his head. By late afternoon it had left the abdomen and became concentrated in his chest. By the evening his chest and abdomen were quiet but his head felt as if it was throbbing beneath my hands. My eyes could not detect any active movement. But at what I would realize later were the actual minutes before death, the top of his head felt as if it was going to explode.

At around 10:00 P.M. I left his bedroom for a few minutes to take a break. About ten minutes later his sister came out and asked me to come in and check on him. As we entered the room she said, "I think he is dead." The moment I saw him I was sure that he was gone, but just to check I placed my hands on his head. Nothing. Flat line. It was incredible. I checked for his pulse, and it was clear that this body was done. It seemed to me that his spirit had been generating energy all day to create the necessary momentum to exit the body leaving through the top of the head.

Amidst the great sorrow of Bill and Lorenzo's sister I felt such joy. Lorenzo was free! I could feel his exhilaration at the accomplishment. It seemed to me that this joy I sensed must be what it is like when there is a birth—the joy of the transition of a soul from one world to the next.

I could tell he was still in the room, and I looked around acknowledging him, but feeling a little funny because I knew he could see me, although I could no longer see him. It would be a few hours before the funeral home people came, and I sensed Lorenzo's continued presence in the room. This was a very difficult time for Bill. Eventually I went home with a mixture of feelings.

In the weeks that followed the tears would come. This precious soul that I only barely got to know had left, and there would be no more for this life. But there was joy as he was released from the burden of this life.

In the future I would learn over and over the joy and sorrow of meeting souls at the end of their current journey and really bonding, only to have to let them go after a brief time. People have asked how I can do this. I can only say that it seems during this time, a person's soul really becomes evident, and to share in the experience on a soul level is such an honor and is so precious that I wouldn't trade it for the world.

It is a continual reminder to me of what we are really made and how personality and possessions are not our whole truth. What is really of importance in this life is not the material and clutter with which we surround ourselves. Nothing much matters in death except the truth of our souls, and to be present when someone is moving from this world to the next gives me a chance to feel that. The veil is very thin in the presence of a dying person, and it is in this place that I feel the closeness of God.

.39.

Not long after Lorenzo's death I went for more formal training in the use of shamanic journeying in death and dying. The work did not seem new to me. I was very comfortable with it. But one piece of information that was relayed by the teacher of the class was very enlightening to me. We were discussing the idea of hospice work and how that evolves for someone. I feel strongly that when someone is meant to do this work it has a way of finding that person. It is not for everyone. In the same way, the work of helping the dead finds a person through out-of-body beings who appear to them—those we call ghosts.

Disembodied spirits appear to people they know can help them. There are no accidents. And as I had been learning through the situation of war, people who die suddenly don't always know to look for the light once they leave their bodies. They become trapped in this plane without a body. It seems that certain people in body can assist those who are stuck, and these "ghosts" seem to know who they are. This information was very reassuring to me because I had been seeing ghosts all of my life.

When I was thirteen my parents and I took a trip to Gettysburg, Pennsylvania, to visit the battlefield there. During this time in my life I was fascinated with the American Civil War. I knew much more about it than an average child would, and it is clear to me now that I must have been involved in that conflict.

We spent a few days at Gettysburg, and each night I was visited by Civil War soldiers, who stood at the foot of my bed.

They said nothing, but they stood there silently in uniform, many with sabers strapped to their waists. I could tell by their uniforms that they were from both the North and the South. I freaked and struggled to stay awake. But I didn't want to open my eyes either; and I was afraid to go to sleep because I thought it was all a nightmare.

There have been other times in my life when I have seen ghosts. But it wasn't until I received the information that they were visiting me because they knew that I could help them that I was comfortable with this. I assume that they were picking up on my soul energy and what it is capable of, but as a thirteen-year-old I had no clue what was happening and their appearance only scared the daylights out of me! Now I can laugh about it! But I spent that entire summer staying up until 3:00 and 4:00 in the morning because I was so afraid to sleep.

.40.

Connections were occurring between the past and the destiny of this current life. But much still needed to be released, and new information continued to find me. One day I was watching another documentary on World War II, this one on the Hitler Youth. I am sure a lot of information was conveyed in this one-hour show but I remember only one thing. Of the Hitler Youth, ninety-five percent joined the SS. As soon as I heard this, the place deep within that resonates with truth went off like a school bell. Whatever else was said after that I no longer heard. I just sat for a while in shock. *There's no point in trying to deny it, is there, Maryanne? No. No point.*

And so my greatest fear became reality. Not only did I deny and hide who I was but I killed who I was. The killing of civilians that I had recalled finally made sense. They had to have been Jewish or some other nondesirable group as defined by the Nazis. In a sad and regretful way it was all beginning to fall into place. And then I realized finally why I hadn't been killed with the rest of my family. It was because the murderers of my family were wearing the same uniform that I wore—the black of the SS!

Not only did this piece of truth add weight to my already-burdened guilt but the feeling of betrayal was too much. I had ultimately betrayed my family! The shield of protection eventually crushed the hostages. No wonder the soldier coming down the stairs after my sister had looked at me strangely but did nothing to me. And no wonder I didn't go back to the army. The very thing I had fought for had killed my family. It wasn't the Russians. They were Germans.

They were the SS. The Schutzstaffel. Hitler's personal police force—the machine that organized and carried out the mass killings of millions. I was a member of the SS! Until that point I had actually started to believe that maybe I could be forgiven, but this! How could I forgive this? At least in some strange way the Wehrmacht seemed innocent, or perhaps naive, in their war against other armies. But the SS! There was no innocence in the SS.

And so it seemed I had reached a point of no return. This was the darkness I had been unable to see through in my journeys. Unforgivable. How could I possibly explain this?

For the next several months I just had to sit with this information and not do anything about it. I didn't know what to think, what to do, so I did nothing.

.41.

That summer I traveled to Mesa Verde, a site in the four-corners area of the Southwest United States that holds ruins of an ancient cliff-dwelling people. It is a series of flat-topped mountains that rise out of the desert. The view from the mesas is like being on an island in a vast ocean of land: you can see for miles.

The people who lived there a thousand years ago, the Anasazi, seem to have disappeared without a trace. No one really knows what happened to them. As I was moving deeper into my shamanic work I had been feeling very drawn to this area. During the few days I spent camping there I felt very much at home. I visited some of the long-abandoned dwellings carved out of the cliffs but the energy of just being on the mesa was what grabbed me. I could feel why these ancient people had been drawn to this magical place; it felt really good to be there.

In dealing with the guilt of being in the SS I began to have dreams about Mesa Verde. I was seeing the people and feeling as if I were a part of that community. It was nice to shift my focus from war and destruction and guilt to what felt like a community of people that lived peacefully together.

One night in a dream I was visited by a man who appeared out of a dark mist. He looked like, and was dressed as, a Native American. He had long dark hair with a few feathers in it. He spoke to me in a language I had not heard before. It was not a long speech—just a few sentences and he was gone. When I woke, the dream was so clear that I couldn't shake it from my consciousness. For the next few days it played back continuously in my mind.

On the third day after the dream, while I was out taking a run, its meaning jumped out at me! This man had spoken in the language of the Anasazi, and he was telling me it was time to go back; it was time to return. Well, I took this literally to mean that it was time to go back to Mesa Verde. But the end of winter was not a good time for me to travel there. So I decided to journey and find out what was being asked of me.

I was guided by my power animal to Mesa Verde. There I saw a small group of people. They were milling around and seemed concerned, disturbed. There was a problem and they weren't sure what to do. One man was asking another for help. It seemed this was the medicine man. He went down into a kiva, a large hole as big as a room dug out of the ground, with a roof and a small opening for a ladder leading down to the floor. Here the men would meet. A few men were drumming, and the medicine man lay down in the center of the floor and appeared to be going into a journey. Slowly I began to see what he was seeing. He had asked what the people should do.

As the information unfolded, I was no longer watching from the outside. I *was* the shaman. The Great Spirit spoke to me and said that we had an agreement that I would return someday, and the time of returning was now.

After a pause, I was told that these people were ready to move on. There didn't seem to be a particular reason. It was just time to leave. They had to go out into the desert. And I heard myself saying, "But they will die if they go into the desert." It didn't matter.

Even though I felt myself doubting, I went outside and told the small group of people the information I had received. They were sad but didn't hesitate. They gathered everything and went into the desert. Life there was very harsh and became increasingly difficult. Eventually they all died, including me. I came out of this shocked and feeling guilty again. I felt responsible for these deaths, and as a result, I did not want to do this work again. *How can I trust the information? People will die! I can't be responsible for this. Being a shaman means being responsible for life and death. How could those people have trusted me? I can't bear that kind of trust. I can't return to this work.*

So now, in addition to being a member of the SS, another lifetime was unveiled where I was again feeling responsible for deaths. What came up for me was the issue of trusting within. I was feeling very doubtful of my inner voice and wanted no part of it. Regardless of my destiny of doing shamanic work, I was not going to be responsible for other people's lives. I had failed too many times. I had given people information that led to their deaths, and I had actually killed.

.42.

I had to move on with my life and my work. This incredible guilt and self-pity seemed like a bottomless pit on my path. Wallowing in it only put me deeper into the hole, and no one but I could get me out.

So I told my story for the first time publicly in a group workshop for healing. It is a powerful thing to place yourself in front of a group of people and tell them of the darkness of your soul. There was a lot of hesitation on my part. I was really scared to publicly declare my hand in death. But I knew that I had to reclaim my power, my truth. I began with the dream of the Anasazi man, and my body was shaking as I spoke. I had no control over it. Everyone in the group showed only compassion; there was no judgment. Without their support I probably would not have gotten through the telling. I told of my guilt that people had died and my fear of the responsibility of the work that I had agreed to come back to do.

The woman leading this workshop, a very unique and gifted soul, looked me straight in the eye and said, "Because of you we died in integrity. We were not murdered by our enemies. We died peacefully on the land and with each other. But it was not the end for us. Look around you. We are back!" I looked around the room. Whether or not these were really reincarnated Anasazi did not matter. The love and compassion in their eyes were all I needed to see that I was forgiven.

I felt some of the weight of guilt fall away, but it still wasn't enough. I had to reveal my Nazi past. I went on, "But I don't deserve this. I killed a lot of people in my last life. I was part of the murder of the Jews." Christine's response was simply, "Every person that I put my hands on for healing is someone that I have done something to in a previous life. And look at me. I have had my hands on thousands of people!"

Oh. Hmm. Christine freely admits her darkness. And yet it is her light that is so obvious. She continued, "We have all been murderers and have been murdered. We have all raped and been raped. We have all been both victim and perpetrator. Part of the healing process of reincarnation is seeing all sides. Eventually all souls will experience all aspects of the human experience if they so choose."

At this point I recalled that in a journey a while back I had asked what had really caused World War II. I had been told it was denial of the darkness. Human beings had been sup-pressing the dark side for so long that the only way for it to heal was to explode. And it wasn't just the suppression that was the problem; it was each individual's unwillingness to see their own darkness within. There is no human soul that does not possess a dark aspect. And all it is asking is that this darkness be brought into the light and then the healing can be conscious and without harm. When the dark side explodes unconsciously it can be very destructive.

This acknowledgment of the dark side of human con-sciousness and my own was a relief. I began to see that all this information was coming up for me to heal myself, and not to make me feel bad about who I am. It wasn't about creating shame but about releasing guilt. And no one was judging me for my past except me!

There is something very healing about standing before a group of people and acknowledging aspects of yourself that you would rather hide. It touched me deeply that these people who hardly knew me could extend such love and compassion. Through their eyes I sensed that maybe there could be for-giveness for this dark part of my past.

.43.

After this group experience I literally felt lighter. It seems that when the energetic field is less dense, more information is allowed through. It is as if a veil has been removed, and the picture is clearer. But for me, even though information would come through, my reaction to it could be another story. I realized why it is so important that information comes through only when a person is ready: it can be very disrupting, even damaging if they are unprepared. But there almost seems to be an inherent safety mechanism within us. I don't think it's any accident when a person doesn't remember a dream or is unable to journey. I trust this to mean that it is not time for them to receive what is awaiting their readiness.

My information was coming through in dreams, too. I had a dream about ghosts. The setting was my home, and my mother was there also. I was walking down the stairs and sensing ghosts all around. I was very frightened. I thought to myself, *it's strange that I should still be frightened by this, as working with ghosts is part of what I do.* Anyway, I was really freaking out and I called out to my mother. She came down the stairs and I started moving towards her. But there was a Civil War soldier standing between us, and I walked right through him. Then I was sure he was a ghost. I was afraid and held onto my mother. And then I heard a voice quite clearly say, "Tell them to go to the light."

I could sense more ghosts in the room and was getting quite panicky. But I listened to the voice and tried to say out loud, "Go to the light!" but it was as if I was paralyzed. I couldn't get the words out. My mouth felt like molasses and my tongue seemed full of novocaine.

The drive to say the words grew in intensity, and I struggled to fight the paralysis of fear until I literally woke myself up screaming, "Go to the light!" I was in a sweat and having a hard time breathing. It was so real. They must have really been here, and hopefully I helped. But obviously I was going to need a lot of practice!

It wasn't long before the next opportunity arrived. Some time after this I had another dream of ghosts. Again the experience was so real that I'm not sure I was really dreaming. The sensation felt like that space between dreaming and waking.

The dream occurred once again within the confines of my home. Off my bedroom where the stairs come up is an over-look to my living room. In this dream I walked out of my bedroom and looked down into the living room and saw that it was filled with people. It seemed as if there were forty or fifty people just standing down there.

They were in neat rows and each one was holding a suitcase. They said nothing, just stood looking straight ahead. Men and women. And then I noticed that the clothes they were wearing looked as if they were straight out of the 1940s: men in overcoats and wide-brimmed hats and women with dresses and coats that came just below the knee. And they reminded me of Jewish people waiting patiently and orderly to be placed on the trains for deportation.

And then I began to lose it. I paced back and forth saying, "What are you doing here? Why are you here? I already feel guilty enough. Do you have to haunt me also?" Then I decided I should reach down and see if my hand goes through their bodies to determine if they are ghosts. And it didn't. They were solid. This freaked me out even more.

I continued pacing and telling them to go away because I couldn't handle any more guilt. Upon waking I felt very uncentered. I wanted this image and feeling of these people to leave. I felt very haunted, burdened.

As the day went by, it finally came to me that these people were here for my help. But interestingly, my reaction of guilt and contrition had left me incapable of functioning the night before. So I put out the call that I would be prepared to assist their going to the light that next evening. Many returned and I drummed and journeyed and used a crystal to assist them in their next step.

This was the biggest group of disembodied spirits I had encountered, and it made me start to think about releasing souls in groups instead of one by one. Doing this individually, it would take forever to help the millions who had died in the war. Then a thought surfaced—*perhaps I should go to them instead of them coming to me.* At that time I began to consider an actual trip to a concentration camp, even though the idea scared the hell out of me.

.44.

I was coming out of the elevator and into my office one day when I saw an attractive woman talking to the receptionist. I had never seen her before, but the recognition bell went off in my head, and I made a mental note that I would like to meet her. As I walked back into my office, my boss said he had just interviewed a new physical therapist that he was going to hire. I knew it had to be the woman I had just seen.

For the first few months, I saw Donna only occasionally. She was going through a difficult time emotionally, I learned later. She wasn't very friendly or open, and we didn't have much of a chance to talk. That was okay with me; I was learning to allow things to go the way they are supposed to. Even though I may be drawn to someone, nothing may happen, so to try to force it is draining. Finally, I signed up for a workshop on craniosacral therapy, and it turned out that Donna signed on for the same workshop.

Craniosacral work is very profound. It is a very gentle mobilization of the cranial bones. When you are experiencing it as the client, it feels as if mountains are moving in you. I was already exploring the possibility of using touch in journeying, and the cranial work catapulted me into this phase.

The first day of the workshop finally allowed Donna and me to spend some time together. We were very comfortable with each other. We learned the techniques working with other partners, but eventually found that we wanted to work only with each other.

This body work was very intense and was bringing up issues for many people including Donna and me. But the more we worked together, the more I was feeling exhilarated; something was happening inside of me. It was a feeling of joy. Walking out of the workshop after the first day, I remember thinking how happy I was to have met Donna. And then the thought that I had been looking for her all my life came in. I wasn't sure what to make of this but found it quite intriguing.

As the workshop continued I found the pull toward journeying growing in strength. I didn't think it was a good idea, though, because there were time limits for each technique and the lights would come on. I didn't want to be somewhere in nonordinary reality when that happened. So I resisted. But each time Donna went to work on me, the pull into nonordinary reality became stronger until I was no longer able to resist.

Towards the end of the second day Donna very gently placed her hands on my head. I became very relaxed and allowed the journey to proceed. I was pulled down a long tunnel, and as I was traveling down a very deep voice spoke to me and said, "Donna is your German sister!" I was flabbergasted. It was such a shock I felt as if I was going to fall off the massage table.

When it was time to get up I attempted to sit up, feeling very shaky and disoriented. Donna asked if I was okay. I said yes but I had just gone on a journey and was a little dizzy. I didn't tell her what had happened specifically and she didn't ask. Donna was interested in shamanic journeying, and we had already spent some time talking about it. But I know I must have looked at her strangely, perhaps as one would look when they see someone they thought had died standing there alive and well, like seeing a ghost.

Another workshop technique involved working around the throat of the client. When I started to place my hands in the position on Donna I was shocked to see a scar across the base of her throat. "How did you get that scar?!" Even as I spoke these words I already knew the answer. I finally understood what had actually caused my sister's death in the last life. Her throat had been cut. In this life she had had her thyroid taken out. But it was clear to me that this scar was an echo from the past.

In the days following the workshop I decided that I'd better get clear about this situation with Donna and so I journeyed. I was taken into the last lifetime to the scene where my family was being murdered in the street. I see my sister lying in a pool of blood. She turns her head towards me and extends her arm to me. As the palm of her hand opens I see a ball of golden light there. She sends it to me. I catch it and bring it to my heart.

My power animal tells me that this golden ball is an essence of soul energy. It is the part of Donna that is capable of deep love. She gave this to me freely to hold for safekeeping until she was ready to get it back. It was now that time. I had been holding this energy for fifty years.

Initially I hesitated about being able to return this to Donna without the help of a third party, but my power animal assured me I could do it. The first thing I did was to retrieve a power animal for her. Then I was told to reach into my heart for the golden ball. When I did this I saw that the ball was not actually in my heart but resting next to it, and I had no difficulty extracting it from myself. As with the power animal, I saw myself journeying to her and blew the golden ball back into her. Instantly I felt relief, as if a huge weight had been lifted.

Over the next few months Donna and I talked and got together a few times. I taught her how to journey and did a soul retrieval for her, knowing that part of what I needed to complete with her was cutting the cord, the attachment from the last life. I found with Donna that we were able to share an initial spiritual connection but the relationship beyond this time would be casual and intermittent. I had to accept that that was how it was and to move on. I felt frustrated though because I was, at that point, looking for friends with whom I could have a spiritual understanding as well as a friendship. This was not to be with Donna at this time.

Initially most of the energetic work I did around the relationship was in the form of journeying—going to Donna's higher self and, with her permission, working from that place. This had an effect because over time the "charge" I felt around Donna dissipated until there was none. This was a sign to me that things were complete between her and me.

An important thing I learned from this was that when I meet someone from my past, no matter how significant or emotional the past lifetime relationship may have been, it doesn't necessarily mean that when we reunite it will be "that person" I have been looking for all my life. Now I can see that there are many souls with whom I have felt a strong bond. And I see now that it was important to meet with each one, to heal what was being asked, and then to move on. If I had attempted to stay very long with any one of them, I wouldn't have been available to the others that were down the road. I believe I have many soul mates and that there is no one soul that I am destined to connect with. There are many choices.

I see more and more now how we are just players in these dramas that keep occurring. We often meet the same souls over and over and switch roles with each other. And it is all about healing the density within our own souls. We pull to us whatever people and circumstances will allow the possibility of healing.

I was prepared to go alone to a concentration camp if I had to, but I had asked the universe if someone could go with me. There were no possibilities among the people I currently knew. Through Donna I met the person who would assist me in my next step.

.45.

A few months later Donna invited me to a party, and there I met Heidi. When I saw her the bell went off in my head.

Heidi was interested in shamanism, and was eager to do some personal healing. We began to spend time together. We were comfortable being together and sharing time. There always seemed to be a lot of laughing and joking. After knowing each other only a few months, we both felt as if we had known each other a long time.

Heidi was a seasoned traveler and not afraid to go anywhere in this world. As the time was approaching for my return to Europe I discussed the trip with her, and she was very willing to go with me. By this time it was clear to me that the destination would be Auschwitz, since this was where the most killing had occurred. I asked her if she was sure she knew what she was getting into. She was sure and had no apparent fear of the destination.

I was curious about our connection and so I journeyed. I was taken to my German childhood and saw that we had been friends from early on. Heidi in that life also had been a male, and it seemed that we were best friends. I was shown a scene of a group of young people sitting around talking and joking with each other. Heidi, Donna, and I were there. My best friend and my sister were flirting with each other, and there was an obvious attraction between them. Heidi and I both had our Hitler Youth uniforms on. It seemed in that time it was pretty hard to find anyone without some kind of uniform on.

140

Then the scene shifted to the Russian front. It's very cold with snow all around. I'm behind a tree. Shots are ringing out, and I get hit in the stomach. I reach down with my hands, and I can see my insides coming out. I want to throw up. I instinctively try to push things back inside. I find myself leaning against the tree and slowly sliding down to the ground. I'm losing strength and everything is getting blurry. I can feel my life waning. A pair of strong hands grab my arms, and I'm being lifted and practically carried. I turn to see who it is and it's "Heidi." He carries me to the aid station where I am attended to. It was the last time I saw "Heidi" in that life.

I then began to see a scene from a previous journey. I was in a field hospital somewhere in the east recovering from the abdominal wound. I'm lying on a bed in a large room filled with the wounded lying on cots. Then there is a lot of shouting, and people are moving quickly. A man dressed in white shouts, "Everyone out!" And soon the sound of explosions from the distance is heard and grows closer. I get up and make my way down a flight of stairs. Several people cannot walk because of their wounds. But we are being pushed down the stairs, and there is no time to help the ones who can't walk. I climb into the back of a truck, and as it pulls away, a bomb falls right onto the hospital. My heart goes out to the ones left inside.

From the truck I am transported onto a train. I am going home to Berlin, and then I see myself in another hospital somewhere in Berlin. Finally I am well enough to go home for a few days before I have to go back to the front. It was during this time at home that I had witnessed the murder of my family.

Slowly the puzzle pieces were falling into place and gaps were being filled.

.46.

And so interacting with Heidi would trigger my last life for me. The feelings of needing to touch it continued. And more and more I felt that the way for healing would be to actually go to Auschwitz. I had to place myself there physically. Only then would I be forgiven.

In the five months prior to the trip to Auschwitz my days were filled with work, reading accounts from the war, journeying and meditating, and when I could, spending time with Heidi. But mostly I couldn't leave the time of fifty years before. It seemed that it was with me in every moment. In fact, I found it difficult to pull myself out of that time and be in this moment.

I read a book called *The Theory and Practice of Hell* by Eugen Kogon that described the concentration camps in great detail. The author had been a prisoner in Buchenwald for most of the war, so he knew what he was talking about.

The book goes into great detail about the different forms of punishment inflicted on the prisoners. The twice-a-day roll call was one of the unique tortures. The evening roll call was the worst. At times the inmates were made to stand for hours in rain and snow, and if anyone was missing everyone had to remain until they were found.

> "During evening roll call on December 14, 1938, two convicts turned up missing at Buchenwald. The temperature was 5 degrees above zero and the prisoners were thinly

clad—but they had to stand in the roll call area for 19 hours. Twenty-five had frozen to death by morning; by noon the number had risen to more than seventy."

When I read this I couldn't help but reflect upon an experience from the fourth grade. There was one boy who always got in trouble in my class. One time as punishment the sister made him kneel in the sun holding his arms out to the side with books in his hands. I suppose it wasn't a very long time that he had to do this, but I remember how hard it was for me to watch him go through this ordeal.

As I read more and more about the cruelty of the Nazis, I tried to comprehend how human beings could do these things. And then I thought, *if nuns can abuse, who couldn't?*

As I read about the daily ordeal I would try to place myself in a prisoner's shoes, so to speak, and I could feel it, perhaps because I was in a prison camp in Siberia and it did strike a familiar chord.

"The camp was awakened by whistles, in the summer between four and five o'clock, in the winter between six and seven o'clock. Half an hour was allotted to washing, dressing, breakfasting and bed making, sometimes an impossible job within that period.

"A number of camps insisted on morning calisthenics, performed winter and summer at break-neck pace for half an hour before the regular rising time. They consisted mostly of everlasting push-ups in the snow and muck. Because of the numerous fatal cases of pneumonia, this practice never persisted for very long.

"Breakfast consisted of a piece of bread from the ration issued for the day and a pint of thin soup or so-called "coffee," without either milk or sugar.

"Next came morning roll call. On a signal the prisoners from each barracks fell in on the camp street and marched eight abreast to the roll-call area. Thousands of zebra-striped figures of misery, marching under the glare of the floodlights in the haze of dawn, column after column—no one who has ever witnessed it is likely to forget the sight. The entire strength of the camp was counted, and this roll call usually took an hour, until it was light enough to work.

"The next command was 'Labor details—fall in!' There was a wild milling about, as the prisoners moved to their assigned assembly points with all possible speed. The camp band, in the winter-time barely able to move its fingers, played merry tunes as the columns moved out five abreast.

"Work continued until late afternoon, with half an hour for lunch, out in the open. In the winter work ended around five o'clock, in the summer, around eight. At the conclusion of the work day the prisoners were marched back to camp, past the band, again ordered to play sprightly tunes. Then came evening roll call.

"Everyone had to appear for roll call, whether alive or dead, whether shaken by fever or beaten to a bloody pulp. The bodies of men who had died during the day, either in barracks or at work, had to be dragged to the roll call area. During particularly virulent sieges, there were always dozens of dying and dead laid in neat 'rank and file' beyond the block formations, to answer the final roll call."

This book was first published in 1950, and estimates of the total numbers of victims have been modified since then. However, the numbers are probably not far off, and the truth will never be known. Kogon estimated there was a total of 7,820,000 inmates in all of the camps from 1933 to 1945. The number of survivors was 700,000.

The overwhelming numbers of people involved and the sheer inhumanity of the Nazis left me drained. And records were kept of everything! The concentration camps really were an industry in themselves.

But mostly I was struck by how nonvaluable human life was. People were just numbers. There was no emotion. How, on a planet where one person like President Kennedy dies and millions are affected, can millions die without people even being aware? Well, after the fact, people were affected by 6 million deaths but in the moment it was happening, not so. It just blows me away that the rest of the world didn't know what was happening. But even people living right next to the camps didn't always know. I think it shows how powerful is the human ability to deny reality.

.47.

To value life and living seems to be one of the lessons of war because life is taken away so casually. In another book about a Dutchman in the German army comes a quote from the poet Rilke.

> *Gieb mir noch eine kleine Weile Zeit: Ich will die Dinge so wie keiner lieben.*
> *Give me but time a little while: I would love all things as none yet has ever loved them.*

Another soldier read this to the Dutchman while they were on a train heading for Berlin. The lines are so beautiful to me and speak of the preciousness of life, especially considering what occurred right after they were shared. The train was delayed in Dresden, and these men became witnesses to one of the greatest tragedies of the war. It was February 1945. Their train was halted in a shunting yard when the air raid warning sounded. There wasn't enough time to get to shelter, so this group of soldiers crawled under the train and waited.

> *As yet a city still lay there, a city with a glittering silhouette of many spires. But from far away came an approaching roar, a roar that swelled to an ominous crescendo.*
> *They came. The first wave of bombers, unhindered by any anti-aircraft defenses, had scarcely dropped its destructive load, when the droning of the next wave could be heard overhead. First a torrent of heavy high explosive bombs, in an unending*

shower. There were blinding flashes. Dry rending explosions, some-times following one another so rapidly that they became one gigantic boom that seemed to come from all directions at once. The ground shuddered. Above us, the carriages were shaking on their rails. Farther away, entire blocks of houses were being lifted up and shifted a few meters, only to collapse slowly, amid clouds of dust.

But it wasn't over yet. More squadrons followed, with a different cargo. Incendiary bombs. Fountains of burning phosphorous fanned out above the ruins in crazy Christmas-tree shapes. In a moment the city was transformed into a seething hell of smoke and flames. Along every street the fire raged and crackled behind windows whose panes had burst asunder. And still they had not done with us. More and more aircraft formations passed overhead, engines roaring, rising to a howl as they shed their loads. Hardly had one carpet of bombs exploded before the next one was falling, starkly outlined against the light of the gently descending flares and of the flames below. The fire sucked all the oxygen into itself; a fire storm broke out. Trees snapped, their crowns tumbling over and over into the flame.

Although we were perhaps half a kilometer away from the edge of the city, at times we had to gasp for breath, and so fierce was the heat that we had to cover our hands and faces. We lay there, so paralyzed by the sight of that all-devouring ocean of flame that it never occurred to us to consider the vulnerability of our own position in this bare shunting yard, an obvious target. It seemed to go on for hours, and perhaps it did go on for hours. At last the heavens became silent again. The bombers had done their work all too well. The all-clear was sounded. Before our eyes the city of Dresden had been demolished.

It was several hours before we were able to go anywhere near the outskirts of that volcano. Orders were shouted. We moved forward with dragging feet.

Small groups of us were directed hither and thither by the civil guard. Once there, we were again shown the maps marked with the sites of air raid shelters. But what was where? In some areas the rubble was two and three floors deep. Nevertheless, we set to work, side by side. With shovels, with picks, with our bare hands, our faces protected by wet cloths. The turbulence was still so great that sometimes the fire came literally rushing around the corner. The air was burning. Stones were burning. Everything was burning. And, unbelievably, there were still people walking about, dazed, covered in burns, in a city bereft of all landmarks.

We toiled from one layer of debris to the next. We were oblivious of the passing hours, oblivious of fatigue. We toiled, lest we should have to see, to feel, to think.

We found no life under the ruins. The air raid shelters had become ovens from which all oxygen had been sucked out by the sea of flames above. They had been overcrowded. Old people, women, children. So many children. There was nothing to do but carry them outside and to lay them side by side in endless rows for identification. That was what we did, with hands that had lost their sense of touch.

Within one day the city of many spires had been reduced to a mass grave. Death was present on such a scale that life, the disparate activity of the blackened rescue teams amid the smoke and rubble, took on a ghostly quality. In squares, in open spaces surrounded by the skeletons of buildings, funeral pyres were erected on railed grids. Infectious disease might break out, rats might be attracted. Burying the bodies was impractical, there were far too many. How many, in a city overflowing with refugees, no one would ever know, not even to the nearest thousand. No one could say how many had jumped into the river Elbe to escape the flames; people who could not swim, people who were injured, mothers with children in their arms; no one could say how many still lay dying, maimed, touched by that terrible phosphorous rubber which, after you thought you had extinguished it, flared up again and only required oxygen to eat its way through everything; no one could say how many still lay buried under the rubble. It was night. Day dawned. Evening fell again. A new day. A night. And another day. Three days and three nights, seventy hours. Then we returned to the railway yard. The city we left behind us was still burning. But there, incongruously, stood our train. Undamaged. We crawled in. There lay our belongings, exactly as we had left them. My kit bag. Willy's kit bag. On top of it, an opened book of poetry:

Gib mir noch eine kleine Weile Zeit....

Give me but time a little while...."

I would read accounts like these and then for hours, reeling from the abuse and disregard of human life that was to be found everywhere, I would be in a daze. Unable to talk. Unable to comprehend.

.48.

I continued journeying and meditating, always feeling impatient that the whole story would not reveal itself to me. I wanted to know it all so I could get it over with. Spending time with Heidi and books I was reading brought up feelings about the past, but nothing really concrete. Still I could feel that I was healing. An excerpt from my journal helps describe this:

> December 8, 1993
> Feelings of familiarity. Deja vu. New friends ringing in the old for me. But again it is nothing specific. Just a feeling.
> Pieces. Little pieces coming together. One by one. Bit by bit. Maybe it is the reversal of the last time where one by one they were lost. And now it returns slowly bit by bit. A time of gradual soul loss to be met by a time of the slow but continual retrieval. Yes, there were actual soul retrieval ceremonies but over time it seems I get fuller. The soul retrieval is like the door opening and creating the permission of soul return but the actual process of parts returning continues for some time. Perhaps a certain threshold amount of soul energy must return with the help of the shaman but once it is initiated more soul energy can return spontaneously, over time.

Again the timing of things and the unfolding of things amaze me. The next piece for me would be a movie. Four months before I would actually go to Auschwitz, the movie "Schindler's List" came out. I knew I had to see it, and I knew that it would be one the hardest things I had to do up to this point. But I thought to myself, *if I can't get through this movie then how could I possibly expect to get through Auschwitz itself?*

Even now it's difficult to find words to describe how this movie affected me. The reality of that time confronts the viewer. I believe that anybody who saw this film would be profoundly affected. I was in an altered state for several days after. I felt touched in a place so deep within me that no words could describe it—it was a feeling of such overwhelming sadness that I felt I might drown.

If I had any doubts of the seriousness of my quest to enter Auschwitz, this movie drove them out. Interestingly, though, my desire to go only became stronger.

.49.

With time, more information came through. Almost every night in the months before the trip I would meditate or journey in my hot tub. But it wasn't just information coming in; I was also in the process of releasing. Each night I would enter the hot tub feeling fairly centered and calm emotionally, and almost always after a while I would tap into a place of deep emotion. I prayed to God for forgiveness and guidance. *Please show me what to do. And I would apologize over and over. I'm so sorry. I can't justify my part but I am so sorry. Please forgive me.* And the tears would come from a place so deep I didn't think they would ever stop.

Along with the release came valuable information. A ritual came to me in one journey, the purpose of which would be to help cleanse the German soul and to ask forgiveness from the victims of the Nazis. I picked some sage from near my house and dried it in the sun. Then through a friend I acquired some soil from Germany. I mixed the soil and the sage together and burned it. This mixture would be taken with me to Poland and sprinkled on the Polish soil as a cleansing.

I was also told to take with me the various crystals I had used in journeys to that lifetime. As a way to move through the darkness I used a crystal as a flashlight, and I found I could move through a dark space and not get stuck in it. I would leave these in Auschwitz for the souls that remain. As I had used the crystals to find my way into the darkness, those that exist in the darkness could find their way to the light by these beacons.

Often my journeys took me to the camps where the work of soul release was already in motion. And the main theme that came up for me was forgiveness. Could I be forgiven for my past? But as I journeyed into this theme I found that forgiveness was crucial not only individually but for all the groups involved.

I found myself traveling into different sections of the camp. One of the places that was the most difficult and disgusting were the mass graves. People were piled row upon row, and I don't think they were all dead before being placed in these pits. They died frightening deaths. One of the things the Nazis did, which is still hard for me to believe, was to drive people, like herds of cattle, into flaming pits, shooting and burning them, while some were still alive.

And of course there were the gas chambers.

But something surprising came up for me. Many of the souls still stuck could not leave when I came to them. There were places where prisoners were still guarded by the SS with ferocious dogs. And I was told quite clearly that until these victims could forgive their perpetrators they would not be released. I was stunned at this because I could see that it was all up to them. The guards and the dogs were an illusion. Through forgiveness these people would be free but they were so filled with resentment and anger they were unable to move from this place. And I began to understand what hell is.

But the need to forgive myself would be the greatest obstacle. The feeling of betrayal that I carried seemed unforgivable. I felt more and more that only by placing myself physically in the gates of hell would I find healing.

And I wanted to know was why all this was happening. Why did I have to go through all of this? I was guided to the beginning of this century, and I saw myself talking with a teacher. I saw myself asking, "How can I truly come into my power in this century?" I was shown some choices, and what amazed me was that I saw how I had deliberately picked the experience of the last life. And what my teacher told me was that it wouldn't be that experience alone that would empower me but the working through of all its repercussions in the next life.

And so I see how I had choices and this was my choice. Next time I think I'll give a little more consideration to the other options before I make a decision!

But this piece really showed me how everything had led to now. My whole life had been in preparation for this time. And I could really see that the only choice was to move forward and move through. I felt as if I were standing on the edge of a cliff where I couldn't see the bottom, and so I just wanted to stay standing for a little while longer before I leaped.

.50.

You'd think by now I would be aware that healing has its own course, and that my plan usually isn't a good predictor of the course of events! I had the idea that just by being in Poland my healing would happen, but it wasn't going to unfold as I expected. Still I had to go to Auschwitz for healing.

I made arrangements for the trip. Heidi and I would fly to Warsaw and then take a train to Krakow, about forty miles east of Auschwitz. We would be in Krakow for several days and somewhere in that time we would take the short journey to Auschwitz.

"Sorrow is like tears that become a river."

These were the words of a Polish poet told to us by a Canadian woman riding with us in the van from the airport to the train station in Warsaw. The poem continued for several more verses, but this was all I remembered and all I needed to hear.

Comprehending just how many tears it takes to create a river is like trying to comprehend 6 million souls. The enormity of Auschwitz is overwhelming. The sorrow of a river of tears is overwhelming. And the notion of responsibility at attempting to carry this burden is almost laughable. But no laughter is heard in a river of 6 million murdered souls.

.51.

Landing in Warsaw gave me the shakes. Bringing myself physically closer to my past always makes me shake. And I remember in shamanism shaking means power. But my shaking doesn't really feel powerful, it feels uncontrollable. I often can't make it stop unless I shift out of whatever I am experiencing. I do know that it happens when truth is moving through me, when information of the last life moves through me. I shook as we landed in Warsaw, as I looked out and saw suburbs with a tainted air surrounding everything and sensed that destiny was calling me nearer to my truth.

Looking out the airplane window, I saw a sky that seemed permanently immersed in a gray thickness. Was it oppression? The air of a city must reflect something of its nature, its consciousness.

The scene was bland. Nothing in particular drew my eye. As I entered the airport the blandness continued. One thing I noticed, though, was that everything was tiled with small tiles such as those on a bathroom floor. But here the tiles continued from the floor and along the walls. They were of a pale color. Perhaps beige. And very clean, almost sterile. It was as if the airport was one big bathroom. And all it had was the bare necessities. No decoration. No plants. No chairs. No resting or admiring the view here. Just get your bag and move on.

A few of the airport employees seemed somewhat excited. This was a new time and there was openness and anticipation at what had been walled off for fifty years. *Who are these people coming from the West? How exciting for us that they are here,* say these people. But I noticed others who are not at all happy with our arrival. They are uncomfortable with these new times, perhaps preferring the familiar routine of the Communist way. Bland and boring as that may have been, it was comfortable. Everyone was the same. Nothing stood out.

One of the first things Heidi and I did upon arriving was to exchange money. At that time $1 equaled 20,000 zlotys, and when we exchanged $100 we seemingly became Polish millionaires! We were actually in another country, but spending money was going to feel like playing Monopoly. Wow, that meal was cheap! It cost us only 300,000!

Except for meeting the Canadian woman, the van ride from the airport to the train station was uneventful. But I saw for just a moment the memorial to the Warsaw Ghetto uprising, a large cemented grounds with cement pillars rising to the sky. It was very powerful, and I felt the time of fifty years before come alive. Until then, what I had read in books or seen in documentaries wasn't real. What I would actually do came to the surface.

We rode past the memorial, continuing toward the station. The street on which we were traveling was shabbily constructed, reminding me of Taiwan. It appeared there weren't even curbs meeting the edge of the street, just dirt somewhere between the sidewalk and the street. Welcome to the third world!

In the train station absolutely no one spoke English. It took us a while to determine which train to catch. Luckily Heidi is a seasoned train traveler, and she was able to figure it out.

We rode first class on the trains in Poland, which didn't mean we were in the lap of luxury, but it did assure us that the compartment would be our own. Except this once, when a flustered and angry man entered the compartment. He looked at us and then said, "Hi." It was obvious to him that we were Westerners.

After taking a moment to calm himself he told us what had just happened—he had been robbed on the bus from the airport.

He was from Poland but now lived in Canada. He hoped to sort things out with the police although he was out $1,000. He told us his name was Peter and that his childhood home was near Krakow, where he offered us a place to stay. But I felt very strongly the need to be in my own space for this trip and Heidi sensed this, too. We thanked him but did not take him up on his offer.

When we arrived in Krakow, Peter hailed a cab to take us to the hotel and made sure the cabby gave us a fair price. He was one of the first examples of how nice Polish people are. It surprised me somewhat that after all the abuse they had been through, they would maintain such openheartedness with strangers.

It was a pleasant day. The sun was shining and the temperature was mild—sweater weather. We checked into the hotel and found our room. It was 1:00 in the afternoon, and even though we had been up for twenty-four hours, we decided to nap for just a few hours and then explore the city.

We awakened into the unique altered state that the combination of sleep deprivation and traveling thousands of miles creates. It was late afternoon but the sun was still high in the sky. We ventured from the hotel on foot.

The sky carried a yellow haze of pollution. In just fifty years the Communists had nearly succeeded in destroying a city that was a thousand years in the making. Ten kilometers east of Krakow is Nowa Huta, a large industrial city erected by the Communists in the late 1940s. It contains a steel works, which continues to belch out a thick smoke that covers the area for miles around, an ecological nightmare.

We wandered the streets for a few hours and were soon tired and hungry. Exhausted from the long day of traveling, we weren't eager to attempt our Polish to order a meal. We passed a few restaurants but were unable to comprehend the menu. As we rounded a corner I was thinking to myself, *Where is a Pizza Hut when you need one?* And lo and behold down the street, extending from the side of a building was a "Pizza Hut" sign! Hallelujah!

Feeling a little guilty, knowing we weren't being adventurous in trying the local cuisine, we made a pact that from tomorrow on we would try only the local food. But for tonight it was pizza and beer! Polish beer!

We spent a few more days exploring Krakow. We discovered the heart of the city—the old town square, Rynek Glowny. It's a wonderful cobblestoned square surrounded by an array of buildings representing architectural history from the tenth century Church of St. Adalbert to the twentieth century tourist shops, with several structures dating from the renaissance. The square was bustling with locals selling their wares, tourists from many nations wandering about shopping, and to our delight, a Peruvian musical group playing their guitars and flutes and dancing.

I found Krakow to be a wonderful surprise. Its people were very friendly and the history the city preserves was to be valued. It had not been open to the West for long, and the innocence it displayed was precious. This gentle city provided me comfort as I came ever closer to physically entering the dark past.

.52.

And then, as described in this book's first chapter, we went to Auschwitz.

.53.

On our return trip to Krakow we had an interesting experience that was, I think, a lesson in lightness. We boarded the train in Oświęcim that would take us back to Krakow in the late afternoon. The only other train back to Krakow wasn't leaving until around 10:00 p.m., and we didn't want to stay that long.

The train stopped at little towns to pick up and drop passengers. Heidi and I found that we were sharing our compartment with another couple from the States, a college-aged guy and gal who were traveling around Europe. They had also just been to Auschwitz. All of us needed some quiet time, and as Heidi attempted to doze, the rest of us were reading.

We stopped at another small town, and the train remained stationary for quite some time. Eventually everyone who had been sharing our wagon got off except the four of us. We were all a little tired and hadn't really noticed an announcement being repeated on the loudspeaker system. Even though it was in Polish, after a while it became apparent that it was the same thing over and over. All of a sudden the train starting moving again, but it wasn't moving forward. It started to head back in the direction of Auschwitz.

Heidi immediately sat up and said she should have realized that, since the message was continually repeating and the train wasn't moving, it was probably telling everybody that this was the last stop. So we sat there a little concerned that we might be going all the way back to Oswiecim. And I began to think, *this really is a nightmare.*

But then the train stopped at the previous little town we had passed through, and so we all got off. Of course we had absolutely no idea where we were. We could see a bus station and decided to head towards it. The other couple went off to see if they could still catch another train.

So here we were in very rural Poland at a bus station where no one spoke English. It was getting late, and all I wanted was to get back to Krakow for a nice dinner and some good Polish beer. At the ticket window the woman did not seem to understand at all what we wanted. We tried to say "Krakow" as Polish-sounding as we could, but nothing was getting through. Then an old man with no front teeth decided to intercede for us. I think he at least understood that we were trying to get to Krakow. Still the woman seemed unsure. But they kept pointing us to the benches at the bus stop. And so we went over there but still nothing was clear. An old woman was waiting there, and Heidi tried talking to her. It seemed that we were at least in the right spot, but when the bus would come we didn't know.

Finally a young man walked into the station. We approached him and asked him if he spoke English, and he smiled pleasantly and said yes. He was very nice and easygoing. We explained our dilemma to him, and he was able to find out when and where we should be to catch the next bus to Krakow. It wouldn't be long, he told us. Then we explained to him what had happened while we were on the train. He just laughed and said, "But this is Poland. What did you expect?!" He told us the trains could change their schedules any time. The look on his face seemed to say it was really all a big joke. Heidi and I looked at each other and began to laugh, realizing that, yes, we were in Poland and obviously we didn't know what to expect!

It wasn't long before the bus came. Finally back in Krakow, we walked to the town square and our favorite sidewalk cafe, where we ate Polish vegetables and fish and drank delicious

Polish beer as we reflected on the day. It wasn't long before we were able to laugh and feel light. The laughter was a release. In this land that had been home to one of the most notorious killing centers, there seemed to be a sense of humor that forced one to keep a perspective or balance—the perspective of knowing that life does go on. And sitting there in the bustling square, we could feel the enthusiasm for life and the joy of just being alive.

.54.

My Auschwitz experience was very intense and heavy, and I knew when I left there that something important had occurred, but I didn't experience the cleansing I had imagined would happen. Entering the gates had only set a process in motion, and it would take a long time for me to fully understand the significance of Auschwitz in my life.

Auschwitz epitomizes evil. Through the fearful use of manipulation, control, and terror, people were encouraged to lose their humanity. And the inmates were clearly not the only ones. I believe that when one loses his humanity he becomes a tool for the darkness.

Auschwitz represents the ultimate in the control of one human being over another. The only place where a prisoner had any control or freedom was in his thoughts. And sleep, if it came, was the only escape.

Control has been a pattern in my life—from controlling what I eat to planning out my exercise routine, to wanting my dog to behave a certain way, to planning ahead and always trying to predict what will happen next instead of being in the moment. By controlling my feelings and trying to control others, I have allowed control to pervade every part of my life.

And so I entered a place of ultimate control in order to heal myself. But I would not find my demon of control in this camp. It had always been within me. I really didn't have to go anywhere to find it. I had only to look in the mirror.

I had made the intention to heal. In shamanism intention is everything. And every intention has energy. The energy you put out to the world will come back to you. For me, physically taking a journey was a way of cementing intention.

And so we who did not die in this place, in the way the victims did, must somehow find a justification to our lives. We have to find our purpose. We have to bring back the light. We—I—who helped the darkness descend must somehow bring back the light. And so I prayed. "Please accept me and allow me to do this work. Please accept what I have to offer. I have left some crystals and a candle. It is all I have for now. I will always be a part of Auschwitz. There is nothing more I can do but ask forgiveness and be a channel for the light."

.55.

The truth of the evil of Auschwitz is not difficult to see. It is there in the buildings that remain...the gas chamber...the execution wall of Block 11...the suffocating prison cells...the standing cells...the barbed wire...the gallows...the human hair woven into fabric...the thousands of spectacles...the children's shoes. Everywhere you turn the evidence confronts you. You could even take home a brick from one of the buildings as a memento. You cannot deny the existence of this place as you stand in the middle of it.

I thought just by entering the gates and walking the grounds, feeling the evil, and invoking the light, that when I walked out I would somehow be healed. But it didn't happen that way. I didn't feel like I did when I walked out of the cemetery in Berlin. Following that was immediate joy and exhilaration. Walking out of Auschwitz I sensed some accomplishment but of what, I didn't know. And the correct word is accomplishment as opposed to completion, for Auschwitz was only the beginning in my quest to confront evil in myself.

I returned home thinking that I was complete with this past-life work and that it was now time to move on with my life. And I knew I wanted a relationship with someone. It had been three years since my last one, and I felt that this was next for me.

I was very attracted to Heidi but she was in a relationship. I thought I had grown beyond this feeling of not being able to have someone love me because of my guilt. But here it was again. I was disappointed in myself, and so I tried to push her away. But she asked why we couldn't just stay friends. There was no reason to stop doing things together. Not wanting to lose her from my life, I went along with this. But it was clear we weren't going to have anything more than a friendship, and it didn't take long for this to have an effect on me.

My feelings were strong, and I could see they would never be met. I didn't know what to do with what I was feeling, so I tried to stop feeling it. But as I tried to push it away, I slipped into a space of such emptiness that my desire for life began to wane. I found myself wanting to drive my car off the road and down an embankment or into a telephone pole. But I thought, *Oh, I have an air bag and it will save me! If I'm going to do this I want to die, not just end up severely injured.* So then I started driving without my seat belt and all the windows open so that I would be thrown out. I thought this would increase my chances of death. It was as if a dark feeling had taken over my spirit.

I was in dire straits. I felt tormented by a desire that would never be fulfilled. I felt no control over these feelings. But the most overwhelming thought was that I felt betrayed by God. I had been told in a journey that when my work in this lifetime was accomplished, the person who would be my partner would appear. I felt done with Auschwitz but things were not working out the way I thought they should.

I became very angry with God. *How could you do this to me? I have been working on this for years! I have felt the pain and the sorrow and the loss. And now here I am right where I started—wanting a relationship with someone who is not available. Has this all just been some kind of a joke?! Am I never to have someone?! What more can I do? What more do you want from me? The loneliness I feel sometimes seems almost unbearable. I can't endure this any longer.*

.56.

And so I told God to fuck off. I took every crystal and significant spiritual thing I had and buried it. I swore I would never do this work again. If, after all I'd been through, this is what I get, then fuck it. And I began drinking brandy and thinking of how I could kill myself.

It was a little scary as I look back because I could easily picture myself cutting my wrists. And I didn't feel any fear about dying. It was as if I was in a hole, and with each passing moment I went deeper. The pain of despair is an emptiness that feels as if it will consume you. It was as if I had no control. I almost felt as if something else was in control of my thoughts, driving me to destroy myself.

All I wanted was for this seemingly endless pain to stop, and I felt that by ending my life it would. And as I look back, the experience of being so close to taking my own life gave me an understanding not previously known. I had had suicidal thoughts before but I had never been this close. It was almost too close for comfort. I hear the judgments made around suicide in this society, but if you have never been close to it, really close, you have no idea of the intensity of the pain of this space. The pain confuses your thinking, and irrational thoughts enter your mind. And all you want is for it to be over, and the only solution you can see from this space is the ending of this life. Judging someone who is in this place for their actions is extremely unfair.

It was as if there was a battle going on within me—a life and death struggle. Light versus dark. But in truth I was not alone in this. In hindsight I know that my spiritual guides and protectors were there supporting me. And my dog Kelly would not leave my side. She is truly a power animal in physical form. But it was as if there was a greater wisdom that knew I had to go through this. It was a necessary step in my growth, and yes, there was the possibility that I might not make it through. But this was important and a chance that had to be taken.

I sat on the floor rocking myself and crying. And then I thought of my mother. I thought about what it would do to her if her child took her own life. My mother's brother had hung himself about nine years before. If I died by suicide it would hurt her tremendously. And the thought of how painful it would be for her stopped me. I decided that no matter how much pain I was in, I would bear it as long as she lived; and if I still felt like dying after that I would give myself that option. This didn't stop the pain, but I decided I would try to find a way through it and just take it one day at a time.

.57.

That night I had a dream. Heidi and I each had a hand on a table, and she kept trying to put her hand on mine, and I kept pulling my hand away. And this scene repeated itself over and over. I had no idea what it meant.

The following Monday I went to work. It was difficult to see clients in my state of mind, but it was also good to be busy and not think too much. And while working with a very sweet older lady, my whole state of mind shifted. She was having a difficult time with getting old. She talked about how it seemed to be just one illness or injury after another. She was feeling very discouraged; old age was not what she thought it would be. Martha was a very kind Christian woman who relied heavily on her faith for strength. But she was so frustrated with all her medical setbacks! In confidence she told me that although she felt a little guilty, she had found herself asking, where was God? Where was God in all of her suffering?

As I listened to her feeling sorry for herself and wondering where God was, just as I had over the last weekend, I remembered the dream I had of Heidi trying to hold my hand, and I realized in that moment that I could no longer close my heart, that I couldn't keep pushing her away. And in that instant it was like the sun coming out after it had been raining for many days. I couldn't control the situation with Heidi, but closing my heart was not the answer.

I walked out of Martha's apartment feeling lighter and happier. I remember joking with her as I left and noticing that

I hadn't laughed for quite a while before that. Whenever I lose my sense of humor it's always a sign. When I am centered and feel my connection to God, laughter seems to come easily. As the days passed I came to understand a little more of what this meant.

When I close my heart, my life force, my lifeline to God, is cut off, and there can be no life, no existence without God. And so the forces that destroy life began to have power over me. And this is my Auschwitz: to lose my connection with God is to become a prisoner of the dark side. I am slowly learning that there is no middle ground in the struggle between light and dark. At some point we have to choose. And part of being human is having the free will to choose. The problem is that often we aren't even aware of the opportunity to choose.

I am beginning to see how free will is a gift from God. It would be so much easier for him if this was not given. But there is no growth in control and manipulation. And what would be the point of no growth? This new understanding has allowed me to see just how much God really loves us. Really loving is to release; and that's scary because things may not go the way we think they should.

So God sits back and allows us our free will and sees us kill each other and abuse each other; but we also have the choice to love each other and be kind to each other. People often wonder where God is and why he doesn't do something to stop all the destruction and evil in the world. I think the truth of the matter is he that isn't ignoring us; he isn't doing nothing. He is praying for us to see that the ability to change is within us. Rescuing us will not save us. We must learn to save ourselves.

And so we have the free will to have God present in our lives or not. What I realized after all this was that God had been there all along. He was just waiting for me to get a glimpse of his light. I began to understand how we create our own prisons. And the patience and compassion and understanding I felt from him still brings tears to my eyes.

.58.

Coming so closely in contact with this dark place inside me concerned me, for it wasn't the first time. A year earlier I had seen how the darker forces confuse people and pull them off their path. I don't judge darkness as evil or something bad; I think its presence allows us our choice of free will.

Several years ago a good friend and I shared an apartment for a brief time. Debbie was someone I trusted and felt I could depend on. We both loved animals, and she decided that she would get a dog. We both bonded with the dog in a very short time and it seemed equally ours. We shared the responsibilities of care including food and vet bills.

Then the time came when I found my own place. I still felt very attached to the dog so Debbie agreed to share her. The dog spent times with me and times with Debbie. It adjusted well and the sharing went on for some time.

But then our friendship began to change, and things deteriorated between us. Debbie no longer wanted to share the dog. Conversations began to seem hostile, and I could literally see a dark energy in the field between us. It was quite cold. Finally Debbie declared that she did not want to continue sharing the dog and that was that. I never saw it again.

I was sad and very hurt. And I began to feel anger well up in me. I wanted to hurt her back as she had hurt me. But I caught myself. I remembered seeing the dark energy and realized it seemed I was face-to-face with something evil. The pain of having something I loved taken from me could have turned to vengeance, but I realized that was all I needed to cross over into the dark side. This had been a test for me.

The thinness of the line between the light and the dark amazed me. And I found myself laughing and thinking, *You almost got me.* And then I heard myself say words that I almost wish I hadn't: "You'll have to try harder than that!" With time I would encounter the darkness again and again, and I suppose it will never stop. There is always another test just around the corner.

I realized, to pass the test I had to let go. So I performed a ceremony to say good-bye to this dog that had been such a gift to me. I was sad for a while, but seeing the importance of letting go and moving on made it a little easier.

In a channeling shortly after this situation I asked about protecting myself from the darker forces and I received this information:

"There is no need to protect. The simple need is to remain connected. And in your connection you are automatically protected. So stay clear in your connection, not losing sight of what you are doing and where you are going. And being distracted by those, who may in innocence or appear to be in innocence, moving you from your destiny.

"And then there is an energetic communication that occurs where the darker forces do try to manipulate through individuals who are vulnerable and susceptible. You see, it is not the individual being dark or evil. It is their vulnerability that does not allow them to accurately ascertain what their actions imply. They wish no one harm but are not completely able to be clear at times in their interactions.

"And thus there are those who will see you being less vulnerable, more self-assured, and want to trip you and take you back to where they feel safe. So the only lifeline that is available is your connection with Great Spirit, to the universal light, to God, to greater consciousness, to the essence of creation—whatever you choose to call this manifestation of energy. That is your lifeline.

"Do not disconnect it and you will need no protection. You will simply be aware and alert. You will notice vibrationally when it is not for your highest good to be with someone. Do not become overly paranoid about this."

"I notice now that I can tell as people are talking to me whether or not they are telling the truth," I said.

"That is the very thing we are referring to. It is a vibrational quality. It's not the words; it's the energy. And to trust those senses and realize when you are in the energy of someone who is not clear in their own energy. And even if it's just in that moment, it is best to remove yourself, and then not to judge that that is forever so. That people change. People grow. People expand. Look at yourself! (Laughter!)

"Give everyone the opportunity you have given yourself without being vulnerable to them when they are in the process of becoming more aware—and in that process still tending to be more manipulative and controlling.

"Just remember you don't have to be protected. You are connected. And just remember not to pull the cord. And how would you pull the cord? By denying who you are. By returning into more unconscious states of awareness. And that's not to say you must always be perfect. Like the earth, there is night and there is day. The ocean comes in and goes out. The seasons modulate. There is ever changing of expansion and contraction. It is the breath of the earth.

"As it is not wrong to inhale and right to exhale, or the reverse, it is not wrong to be open or to contract. It is the breath of life. It is the rhythm of life. But to hold one's breath and not allow the rhythm, the flow of the life force to move through, does kill. It terminates life.

"And so energetically do not get stuck in your depressions and your elations. Move through them. Flow with them. Breathe into each moment. Breathe into your losses. Breathe into your lessons. Breathe into your joys."

.59.

My dream of the hands began to recur. And now Heidi's hand was on top of mine and staying there. I kept thinking it meant we were supposed to have a relationship; but we didn't and I was very frustrated with this dream. For a few months I had the dream at least once or more a week.

Finally I began doing energy work with a woman named Charlene. She informed me that hands in a dream represent power. And I saw how, by allowing my hand to be taken over by Heidi's hand, I was losing my power. I was losing control. Seeing the deeper meaning of this, I wanted to let go. I didn't want to be losing my power, and so I changed how I was with Heidi. When I wasn't fully in my power I would catch myself and stop giving it away. The dream never happened again. This was an important lesson for me. But still, my lesson in power loss was not over.

For the next year Heidi and I spent time together when we could but it would never be enough for me. I found my feelings for her only growing but she was still in another relationship. And she was also very clear with me that she wanted no more than a friendship. It was not good. I kept wanting to end it but something would come up, usually a trip somewhere that would need completion, and so we would continue. But again I found anger and frustration about her partner.

After a while I became disenchanted with just about everything in my life. I became very burned out at work; it was a drain. I had difficulty getting through the day and couldn't bear the thought of trying to do it again on the next day. I thought about quitting my job but didn't know what I would do to make money. Then I thought about moving. Maybe a change of scenery would help.

I had become so dissatisfied with my life I decided that moving was a good idea. I got really excited about the possibilities. I shared my enthusiasm with Heidi. She wasn't too happy about the idea, but I know she supported me in my choice.

Not long after this she suggested that I come live with her. She had just bought a nice house in the mountains, and it was very peaceful and beautiful. We were sitting on her deck in the warm sun of a spring day, and it was awfully hard to say no to the idea of living there. We talked about what it might be like and both of us seemed excited. We had a really nice day together, and I left her house thinking how much I loved her.

The need to leave faded, and I got very excited about living with Heidi. But then I didn't hear from her for a week. The next time we talked she seemed cold and distant. Her partner was still there, and we would not be able to see each other for a little while. It was clear that her partner still came first. My feelings were hurt. I became increasingly angry and resentful towards her partner.

I became angry every time Heidi and I would plan something that was dashed by her friend's presence. I wanted this woman to be gone. But it wasn't happening. One more time our plans were changed, and it was the last straw for me. Something inside of me snapped and said *this is it. No more.* I felt as if I didn't want to ever see Heidi again, but I did commit to getting together once more and decided to stick with it. And in hindsight it is really good that I did.

I met with Heidi at her house but my mood was already set before arriving. I didn't really want to be there but I thought I would see how things would go. She tried to be light and funny to shake me out of my serious mood. But I wouldn't be budged. I wanted to stay centered and observe what happened. I was almost detached.

At one point Heidi and I were conversing on her sofa, about what I don't really remember. But I will never forget the look in her eyes and the feeling in my body. She was smiling at me but there was no warmth behind it. It was cold. It almost seemed as if Heidi had left for a moment and someone else was in her body. I felt as though I was eye-to-eye with the devil. I was in shock. And the reality of the bigger picture hit me at once. The dark side once again had me in its grasp. My resentment of her situation and her partner was about to pull me into the dark side.

I couldn't leave fast enough. All the way home I kept saying, "Oh my God, Oh my God!" over and over. "Oh my God!" Everything in the past six months made sense. Once again I had lost my connection to God and my higher self. Once again I had let myself be distracted and strayed off my own path. And I was about to cross the line again with all my energy and anger directed at Heidi and her friend.

That night I lay awake amazed by how I had nearly lost myself and the hatred I had experienced—the contempt.

.60.

But it wasn't long before I realized that it had nothing to do with Heidi or her friend. There was no hatred in Heidi for me. The source of hate was me. The hatred was from me and it was for me. Heidi was just my mirror, probably hardly even aware of what she had shown me. And in the wee hours of that morning I sat in my bed in the darkness and realized how much I had hated myself all of my life; how much contempt I have had for myself all of my life; how there was a part of me that was never going to allow me to feel loved; and how I have turned this hatred outwardly towards others.

I realized that when I am in pain I want to get angry. I want someone else to hurt. I want revenge. I want to do anything but feel that loss, that sorrow of feeling unloved. And in the darkness of that night I decided that it was time to stop. I saw how much energy it takes to hate. I don't want to hate anymore. I want to love. And loving takes courage because you must release. You must let go of what it is you want the most. And so I have found myself asking God for the courage to love.

I realized that in trying to get what I wanted the most, I was diverted from my destiny. And maybe that is how evil works. It creates an illusion that if you don't have what you want—that house, that car, that job, that relationship, that money—you will never be happy. And you get so caught up in trying to get what you want that you forget why you are here in the first place.

What I found was that in trying to attain things I wanted, I was the most unhappy I had ever been, and the most disconnected from myself.

I became more aware of my thoughts and feelings. How I felt about my life became apparent to me. I would become angry or depressed when things were not going the way I might like. I decided that I wasn't going to put myself down anymore for not having a relationship. I wasn't going to tell myself that I am a piece of shit and no one could love me. I would love me. I finally decided to love myself. The abuse must stop. If I have to spend the rest of my life alone, I will accept that and not abuse myself or anyone else because of my loneliness.

I wonder if there is actually any evil outside of ourselves. I saw such evil in me, and I needed to see it. Unconsciously keeping this in the dark was only going to damage me and others in my life. I realized how I came in to life with this evil. I died in the snow hating myself for having let my family die, and I would never allow myself to feel love again. It would be my punishment—self-inflicted. From the day I was born I have pulled people towards me who would mirror guilt, hatred, and betrayal of self. But it was finally time to stop. No more. Enough.

.61.

In the midst of all this the federal building in Oklahoma City was blown up. President Clinton was heard to say that we must rid ourselves of evil if this kind of thing is to be stopped. And I see how each one of us is ultimately responsible for this murder as long as any one of us holds an ill intention towards anybody, including ourselves. As long as individuals refuse to see that each one of us holds an aspect of the group darkness it will explode in our faces. That dark aspect in us wants to heal, wants to find the light. We are so numb, it seems, that it takes extreme circumstances to awaken us. It did me. Seeing the darkness of my own soul face-to-face scared me.

Now my feeling of commitment towards God and my destiny is stronger than ever. No person, no possession, no money can compare with the peace I have felt from asking God and love to be in my life and feeling his presence and compassion and understanding and wisdom. And I ask each day—I pray each day—for God to teach me how to love. Teach me, show me. I have spent so much time learning how to manipulate, control, and hate. All I want now is to love and feel peace.

And now I am beginning to feel a love for myself I've never known before—an understanding and compassion and, finally, forgiveness. I see myself as the German soldier, and I just hold and comfort myself and tell myself it's over. The war of hatred and betrayal within me is finally over. And for the first time he looks really good. He doesn't look as though he's just been in a battle anymore. He looks healed and at peace.

It is clear to me now that I did not have to go to Auschwitz for healing. Everything that needed healing was within me from the beginning, and everything I needed to create healing was within me all along. Auschwitz simply represented to me the hatred and contempt I have held for myself. But I was so blocked from seeing this that I needed a mirror as big as Auschwitz to see into the darkness of my own soul.

.62.

Heidi was another mirror. Heidi, my best friend, who saved my life on the Russian front, once again came in to teach me what my life is about at this point. A triangle was the perfect setup for betrayal and mistrust and ultimately hate, all of which I have carried within me. Heidi went with me to Auschwitz, but it was another year before I saw the mirror in her eyes of the hatred within my soul.

And so the answer is to love and release—to know on a deep level that I am lovable and that I deserve love. This could never happen until I loved myself. Each person in my life was just trying to gently show me that I wasn't loving myself, but it took a long time before I could see this. I do now. And the words of my first channeling come back to fulfillment:

> "The solution is universal love. The solution is alchemically to take denser matter and to fill it with light and to create lighter matter.
>
> "And this you must do in your emotional body in regard to the devastation of your country, of your city, of your ideology, of the essence of freedom within yourself. And this freedom must come from within. And this love from within. And this forgiveness from within."

To realize this has been healing. My soul has drawn each experience to me. It could not have been any other way. All the anger and resentment of relationships not working out falls away. The feeling of freedom within me is the greatest gift I have given myself. All the density I have been holding onto is released, and I feel as if the world is at my feet and the possibilities are endless. I see how I had created my own prison. I felt so trapped by my desire for relationships that I was miserable. All along, the truth of the desire was for a loving relationship within myself. The love of God has been there all along.

I started realizing how much my attitude about life has tainted it. I realized that my response to life has been rather immature at times: for example, thinking that because one particular situation isn't working out the way I want, it never will.

When things are going well it is easy to keep a good attitude and feelings positive or light. But as soon as pain comes up or situations do not flow I get cranky, like the little kid who throws a tantrum to try to get her way. I'm beginning to think that at some point I have to stop acting like a kid in response to life's circumstances.

.63.

I have come to understand that I have a choice in how I respond to life. This reminds me of a book that I read several years ago called *Man's Search for Meaning* by Victor Frankl. The author, a trained psychiatrist, was a prisoner in Auschwitz. His observations of camp life from his professional viewpoint are invaluable.

From his book I came to understand that the key to survival—and therefore existence—was not physical ability, but a person's inner attitude and strength. In the prison camp everything could be taken from a person but one thing, their choice of attitude. I came to realize that even when faced with death we still have choice. Frankl wrote:

> "We who lived in concentration camps can remember the men who walked through the huts comforting others, giving away their last piece of bread. They may have been few in number, but they offer sufficient proof that everything can be taken from a man but one thing: the last of the human freedoms—to choose one's attitude in any given set of circumstances, to choose one's own way.
>
> "And there were always choices to make. Every day, every hour offered the opportunity to make a decision, a decision which determined whether you would or would not submit to those powers which threatened to rob you of your very self, your inner freedom; which determined whether or not you would become the plaything of circumstance, renouncing freedom and dignity to become molded into the form of the typical inmate.

"Seen from this point of view, the mental reactions of the inmates of a concentration camp must seem more to us than the mere expression of certain physical and sociological conditions. Even though conditions such as lack of sleep, insufficient food and various mental stresses may suggest that the inmates were bound to react in certain ways, in the final analysis it becomes clear that the sort of person the prisoner became was the result of an inner decision, and not the result of camp influences alone. Fundamentally, therefore, any man can, even under such circumstances, decide what shall become of him—mentally and spiritually. He may retain his human dignity even in a concentration camp. Dostoyevski said once, 'There is only one thing that I dread: not to be worthy of my sufferings.' These words frequently came to my mind after I became acquainted with those martyrs whose behavior in the camp, whose suffering and death, bore witness to the fact that the last inner freedom cannot be lost. It can be said that they were worthy of their sufferings; the way they bore their suffering was a genuine inner achievement. It is this spiritual freedom—which cannot be taken away—that makes life meaningful and purposeful."

Over and over I have seen in my physical therapy work a range of attitudes in response to life's challenges. I have seen people dying of cancer who were very clearly in physical pain but whose burden was not apparent. And others who were experiencing something like a broken ankle were very much weighed down by their suffering.

I see that we have a choice of becoming a victim of circumstances and therefore disempowered and stuck, or we can become empowered by our circumstances and evolve to another level of consciousness.

Ultimately we are always left with at least one last choice. I may not be able to change the external circumstances of my life but I have control over my attitude. And to take on depression, misguided anger, or hopelessness is, I think, to invite death.

The control I exert over my attitude about my life has been one of the main changes that has occurred with the healing of my past life. Through awareness of my ability to control my inner world, I work each day to bring peace into my life. Some days I actually feel happy, and others it is more a feeling of contentment. But the key has been to try and meet my own needs—to love myself no matter what is happening around me.

I have seen people in my hospice work who finally find peace just before they depart. I am trying to find that peace in myself each day.

.64.

So what does it all mean? How am I different? For one thing, I feel a peace inside that I've never known before. I respond to situations with more maturity. I feel more whole. My female and male aspects are in a healthy balance. I finally feel safe in allowing my feminine side to come out, and I have faith that my male side will always protect me. Hans, my male aspect, is with me. All the energy he felt for trying to get himself and his family through a horrendous time is with me now. But now we don't have to hide or betray or lie.

The obsession that was with me for years of needing to read and watch anything and everything that I could about the war in Europe has left. I am surprised at my reaction when I see a book about the war. I still look at it for a few seconds. I might even pick it up and open it, but the feeling in my body tells me there is no longer a pull. It's almost like falling out of love. The attraction just isn't there anymore. But there is no sadness in letting this go; it is a huge relief.

I find it curious to consider how all this happened to me in Utah and how I ended up here. After living in Hawaii for fifteen years, I left to attend physical therapy school. I had applied to several schools, and Utah was my last choice. God was not going to give me an option on this one. Utah was the only place I was accepted. It was my destiny to go there. There can be no accident that it was in Utah that I met so many of the people from my last lifetime. Many of these people were transplants to this area and came for various reasons, but eventually we found each other.

Now I sit back and wonder at how long this process took. Six years! I had to go through six years of hell. My memories began in May of 1989. The actual war had began in September of 1939. I finally felt the forgiveness within myself on May 8, 1995—fifty years to the day from the end of the war in Europe, VE Day! I can't believe that I had to live through that war, die, come back, and go through it again! But that is what has happened to me. It is still so close to me that as I reread what I have written the tears flow. The emotion is still present; but at least I now know it is over. Finally I feel the freedom from within. I see that owning my darkness within myself is actually the key to freedom.

C.G. Jung said, in 1945, "One does not become enlightened by imagining figures of light but by making the darkness conscious. The latter procedure, however, is disagreeable and therefore not popular."

To make the darkness conscious requires honesty. Honesty within the self, about the self, brings integration and wholeness. Seeing the whole picture—the whole self—is the key. There would be no healing for me until I could accept that I had been in the SS and had participated in killing. Healing came through an honest dialogue with myself about my own darkness.

When we are unable to see the truth of our own soul, whether consciously or unconsciously, we are being dishonest. The result is a disintegration or split in our soul energy. Whenever we lie to ourselves, we lose a piece of our soul.

I have been able to find contentment in each day, whether or not people are around me. I simply accept whatever comes my way and thank God for each day. This is very different for me. Previously I would not have been happy alone. Now I feel that God is guiding me, and whatever comes my way must be what I need. Rather than having a rigid plan of what I think should be, I use whatever is present.

I feel more energized than ever. Sometimes I feel my soul is rotating and spinning as if it's on caffeine, vibrating from deep within me. Despite the fact that I have nights when I can't sleep because so much energy is coursing through my body, I get up the next day ready and refreshed. This is definitely a new me; the old me needed a lot of deep sleep.

One of the keys to the final phases of this healing was releasing not only the guilt and hatred from the previous life—it almost feels that I have released my entire existence to this point. I have a sense that my life has just barely begun.

.65.

To create the space for my new life a cleansing was needed—I had to clean out my house. Although this was a physical process, it was energy that needed to be released. I had boxes of things accumulated over the years that had been sitting in a closet—letters and mementos from old friends and lovers, trophies from athletic competitions, academic awards. I was obsessed with removing these from my space; they no longer belonged here. And in the midst of my rummaging I found a personal check from a friend that I had not thought about for many years.

I met Barbara twelve years ago when I first moved to Utah. I lived in the graduate dorm on campus for the first year, and I met a lot of people there including Barbara. She was rather shy and quiet and a little older than I. She was quite a bit overweight, and I noticed she would get short of breath easily. Her goal in life was to become a doctor. At this time she was working on a graduate degree in one of the sciences. We would often sit together in the cafeteria for lunch or breakfast and talk. She was very interested in understanding the human body and was curious to know what I was learning about it in physical therapy school.

As I got to know her she told me that she had had medical problems all her life. She had been in hospitals several times and almost died more than once. I was amazed that she was here trying to go to school. It was clear that she wasn't well physically, and it was a struggle for her just to walk from one class to another. But there was an inner strength urging her towards her goal.

I had an old paperback version of *Gray's Anatomy*. I had to buy the hardback for school, and I wanted to give her the paperback so she could pursue her interest more. She had insisted on paying me. I simply wanted to give it to her but we finally agreed that she could pay me $3, and she wrote out a personal check in very shaky handwriting.

The following January Barbara died. She simply did not wake up one morning. Her roommate had gone to class and came back to find her still in bed, cold. We were all shocked. Obviously she was much sicker than any of us realized.

At that time in my life I had had very little experience with death and was greatly affected by her loss. I had been her closest friend in the dorm.

A few days after she died I was sitting at my desk in my dorm room trying to study but to no avail. I had a feeling to look towards the closed door of my room. When I did I saw Barbara standing there. I couldn't believe my eyes. She stood there for a few moments looking peaceful and serene, saying nothing. And then she was gone.

When this happened I seriously questioned the truth of my eyes. As I look back now, I have no doubt of the truth. And when I looked at the check she wrote I smiled. Barbara was trying to give me a message about where my life would take me. At the time I had no clue. And maybe she was also saying thanks for being a friend. And again I am reminded of just how precious each moment is, each interaction. A small act of kindness can mean so much. A precious soul can be gone in the blink of an eye. To have missed an opportunity to share is truly regrettable.

When I think of Barbara now I thank her and know that she is okay. I know that even though her life was short, she met her destiny and that it was her time to depart. She reminds me of the man I met on the train in Germany—an angel with a message. And I see how I have been blessed and guided all along. It took me twelve years to fully understand Barbara's gift, and I won't forget her again.

.66.

Another change in my life has been the desire for daily prayer. I have always heard about the power of prayer but never really believed it. It reminded me too much of something that I was told to do as a child. But now it is something that I want to do. Maybe that's the difference. Maybe that's where the power is—it has to come from within.

I talk with God often throughout my day but I also have a few special places in nature that I like to visit. It makes my prayers seem a little more formal and more intentional if I make the effort to travel to a specific place to meet with God.

One of these places is in a field not far from my home. There is a stream with a beaver lodge surrounded by aspen trees. When I enter the trees it feels as if I have entered a holy place. I like to sit by the rushing waters of the stream and talk to God. The amazing thing about praying there is that I can really tell that God is listening. More and more I am getting answers to my questions. It's almost too easy and obvious.

.67.

I had been praying for release and love and so was led to the next step. Another object that I found in my cleaning frenzy was a ring that my first lover had given me. I thought I had already let this go and was surprised to find it in my possession. That first relationship had been very sweet and tender, and I allowed myself some time to remember those feelings. Then I remembered the separation that was so painful that it became the trigger to begin my inward searching. I see now that it was necessary and how that pain was a gift. But I now have the wisdom of knowing that I never have to go through that again. So I found myself thanking Jane from the bottom of my heart and sending her love and light, and hoping that her life is unfolding in the way that she wants.

Holding the ring in my hand, I saw that it represented to me the full circle of my journey—everything that I had been through in the last twelve years, every relationship from Jane to Heidi. Each one had tried to show me in some way how I wasn't loving myself. Each one had loved me and gently tried to open my eyes. It occurred to me that my lesson of self-hatred could have been much harder. I could have pulled people towards me who might have been harmful.

Now I see how important each person was and how the pain of each breakup was part of the process for me. Any residual anger I held towards them now fell away. I had created it all. I had pulled people to me that would help to bring out something within myself that needed healing. There was no way around it. I came in with self-hatred, and holding onto it would prevent me from moving forward. I had to come to this point, this place in my life where I had to release everything, including my friend Heidi. This would bring much sadness to me, but I knew that I had to let go of her also.

I decided that I would perform a ritual with the ring to represent the release of all these people and the pattern that accompanied them. A ritual is only as powerful as the intention and feeling one puts into it. The deeper I was willing to go with my heartfelt emotions the greater the release would be.

I went to the beaver stream and held the ring in my hand. I asked God to help me release and voiced aloud what the ring represented to me. I thought of each person and how much I had loved them—how wonderful it had been to feel love and how painful it had been to lose them. I knew it was important to feel all the feelings. And I had absolutely no regrets. I was grateful to each one, for without them I would never have reached this place of healing. I thanked them from the bottom of my heart. I released them one by one in love and light and asked God to watch over them.

I then asked that whoever found this ring again would know only love and healing. I tossed the ring into the energized waters of the stream that was filled with the spring runoff. And I realized how appropriate it was that into the water that had been held as snow for many months in the mountains I was releasing what had been held for many years in my heart. Emotions from deep within me surfaced, and I cried my grief and sorrow. But for the first time I noticed that I could feel this deep emotion without losing myself in it. Soon the emotion passed, and I felt light and released. I thanked God and all my spirit guides.

This led me to the issue of emotion about the past and how I am now. If I choose, I can allow myself to feel the sorrow of the loss of my German family and Berlin, old Berlin. But I no longer feel like it overwhelms me, takes me over. I feel more control. Yes, it is there and will always be, but at some point you have to move on. And so I was told that as the purpose of war is control, the answer is to release. "For what was is no longer. Let it go. And in this you will experience great freedom in your spirit."

And so this journey began for me with a soul retrieval. But the process of truly becoming whole involved years of remembering a past filled with darkness and loss. Slowly I have moved through, and I now feel that I have found the light and am at peace with my past. And what I have been telling my clients—in body and out of body—about going to the light has also been true for me. I've heard it said that we teach what we most need to learn! I know how scary it is to be in the dark and have no sense of direction, but I do believe that if we intend to find the light we will. The power of one's intention should never be underestimated.

When you reclaim your soul you no longer need something from someone else. The addiction is over. And it becomes easier to allow others their choices even if that choice is not you. I placed incredible pressure on myself because of my actions and experiences of living through Nazi Germany. But I don't think the purpose of it all was to live for years with guilt and sorrow. I think it was to reach deep inside myself for healing. And I have found a place of more compassion and love and forgiveness than I ever knew was possible. I think the truth is that I have found God—in myself—because now I feel that I am okay.

.68.

My realizations of the meaning of Auschwitz and God in my life were profound and seemed to solidify the purpose of my six-year process of self-discovery. Much of my healing was the releasing of each person who had been a part of the unfolding process. I felt complete with the release of all of my soul friends except Heidi. I knew when we went to Auschwitz that she was one of the final pieces in my healing. Yet she continued to be an important part of my life, and I found that perplexing. When things were completed between myself and my other soul mates, they were no longer an active part of my life. But Heidi was still there, and I very much wanted her to be.

I became concerned that her continued presence in my life somehow represented that I wasn't finished with the work on this past life, and I was frustrated with that possibility. I wondered if I simply needed to do more release work around Heidi.

With the assistance of Charlene I went into a meditative space to release Heidi from my life. The depth of my emotion that surfaced at the thought of really letting go of Heidi surprised me. As Charlene worked energetically on my abdominal area, the tears came and soon grew into sobs. Within a few moments the thought of leaving Heidi was replaced with the memory of leaving my family in the burning city. Charlene asked if I had ever forgiven myself for leaving them. I thought I had forgiven myself for everything including abandoning them, but as soon as she said this I realized how guilty I felt in the actual moment when I made the decision to walk away. How much I wanted to return to the city to save them, to bring them back, to be there for them. But it wasn't to be. They had already met their fate, and there was nothing I could do.

This brought up a memory from early in my current life when I was about six years old. I was home with my mother. The scene was very vivid in my mind of talking with her while she was ironing some clothes. I told her that I would never leave her. She smiled and said something like, "Honey, that's nice but you will." I tried to say, "No, Mommy, you don't understand. I mean it! I will *never* leave you!" It was a very strong feeling inside of me. I realize now from this perspective that, standing on that hill in Germany in 1945, I made the decision that I would never leave anyone I loved again.

My healing process had begun with a feeling that there was something missing from my life. My search revealed a family that had been destroyed by hatred. There were emotional scars that carried through into this life after witnessing the murder and yet having to continue on with that life—my guilt at not dying with them and my guilt of leaving them in the city.

But I did leave them. And that was exactly what was supposed to happen. But in that moment of guilt I had lost a part of my soul. And I came to believe that every time I released someone from my life I would never see them again. Many times that was true. So I have had the pattern of holding on and trying somehow to be there for the other person even when relationships were well over. Now I realize how many times in this life I have stood on the hill looking down at the burning city and have gone back in to hold on and be there for just a little longer, even though all around me was dying.

What destiny brings souls together? It seems that when we release the ties that bind, the truth of a situation or relationship is able to come through. My work around the final letting go of Heidi came to represent the family that I needed to release so that we could all move forward and continue on our soul's paths. My German family had died fifty years ago, and the final piece of healing for myself was to actually say good-bye. I had forgiven myself for everything, but I had never said good-bye. And now I realized that until I could say good-bye, there would always be a cord connecting me to them and that life. It is no longer for my highest good to remain connected. It's time to move forward in this life. And in my release from them they are now released from me. We can all go on to what is next.

The idea of having to leave those we love behind is a difficult and sad task but necessary for growth. I have realized the only soul that I have any control over is my own; I cannot save anyone but myself. In the end each soul must save itself.

Included in this releasing was letting go of the energy between Heidi and me from the last life, and the gift that I was given in return is that she is still a part of my life now. With a sense of new energy coming into each of our lives, we are moving on, exploring life and new adventures.

People come into our lives for different reasons, and the intensity of the attraction is not necessarily an indicator of the longevity of the relationship. It may be more an indicator of the urgency of healing what is necessary for lives to move forward. When the healing is complete we each move on. Then there are those who come into our lives not for healing the past but for something we have chosen to learn together in the future. But it is only through release that the truth can be known.

So now once again I am standing on the hill looking down at the burning city, knowing that there are people I love in that city and that they need healing and love. I ask God to be with them and to help them find the love within themselves. And finally I say good-bye to the Grunewalds and turn and walk away.

.69.

At long last my soul is at peace with this German lifetime. I feel healed. I no longer have any desire to look back at this life. I had the sense when this all started that I didn't have much choice in pursuing the truth of this past life. Now it is even clearer how necessary it has been. The unfinished business of my last life would not allow me to move forward in this life. But now it is finished, and I am moving forward and looking ahead.

The need to explore past lives may not be for everyone. I think the purpose of this life is to grow by living in the here and now. But if something from a past life is incomplete, a person may have difficulty living this life effectively and fully. They may need to look back. I think each individual will have a sense of whether or not they need to do that.

Now my life is filled with optimism for the future. I am excited at the thought of new experiences and people coming my way. Finally I can look forward and really begin the work of why I am here on this planet at this time. I feel the call of the earth mother crying out. I have a sense of urgency for her healing and our healing. I want to be part of that process.

I hope that through my own healing process, some healing has been extended to others. Those souls carrying a similar energy to mine may learn from my process rather than suffering as I have. I have been told that one aspect of the social healing process is that one person moving through the steps of the healing can act as a proxy for the group. I hope that in some way my work will help heal some of the wounds of the holocaust.

My thoughts rest with all the victims of fascism. And in my heart I pray that Germany's burden has been lightened and the human race can move forward. I was told in a journey that as Berlin goes, so goes Germany; and as Germany goes, so goes the planet. May God guide us all.

Author's Note

Throughout this unfolding six-year process, I have made attempts to find an actual record of Hans Grunewald and/or his family. Each time I researched, I came to a roadblock of records not being available until 100 years after their deaths. I'm hoping it may still be possible to find something about the Grunewald family in Germany. I will continue my search.

Hampton Roads Publishing Company

. . .for the evolving human spirit

Hampton Roads Publishing Company
publishes and distributes on a variety of subjects,
including metaphysics, health, complementary medicine,
visionary fiction, and other related topics.

To order or receive a copy of our latest catalog, call toll-free,
(800) 766-8009, or send your name and address to:

Hampton Roads Publishing Company
134 Burgess Lane
Charlottesville, VA 22902